Go For It!

AF797630

Go For It!
How Anyone Can Achieve Their Dreams

Donna Dick Connor

All Rights Reserved. No portion of this book may be reproduced, stored in a retrieval system, or transmitted in any form or by any means-electronic, mechanical, photocopy, recording, scanning, or other-except for brief quotations in critical reviews or articles without the prior permission of the author.

Published by Game Changer Publishing

Paperback ISBN: 978-1-961189-43-0
Hardcover ISBN: 978-1-961189-44-7
Digital: ISBN: 978-1-961189-45-4

DEDICATION

This book is dedicated to my family…

Jeff…

You support me even when you don't understand my drive or ambition, and I can't thank you enough for allowing me to simply be me and supporting me as I go after every goal and dream I have — and those I keep coming up with.

Kailee, Kaitlin, and Willis…

You three are the BEST kids a mom could ask for! I am so proud of each of you and the adults you have become. Thank you for your love, support, and especially the laughs.

I pray you will continue to always pursue your goals and dreams with gusto.

Read This First

Just to say thanks for buying and reading my book, I would like to give you a few free bonus gifts, no strings attached!

To Download Your Free Gifts Now, Visit:
www.go.lifeonpurposeacademy.com/GoForItBookGifts

Go For It!

How Anyone Can Achieve Their Dreams

Donna Dick Connor

Foreword

Every so often, a book comes along that appears simple, straightforward, and seems not too different from other books out there, only to realize once you get into it that there are gems of wisdom in it that can change your life — if you act on them! This, in my opinion, is such a book. Donna Connor includes valuable principles in this work, which, when interwoven with other principles she covers, can take on a new and powerful meaning.

I find Donna's writing style and her entire demeanor to be expressive and impacting to the degree that people in her sphere will be inspired to action. This is a rare and desirable trait that you, as a reader of this book, can profit from as well. Dr. Phillips Brooks once said, "Few things are more powerful than the contagion of a victorious personality!" That's Donna, described to a tee!

Go For It! will take you to a new level of achievement if you put the ideas into practice. Early in the book, she touts the importance of establishing goals, visions, and dreams. I agree wholeheartedly with this principle of self-direction. She further establishes the principle of having a positive mindset. She believes that mindset precedes skillset, for it is with a determined mind that we vigorously seek education and ideas that can be life-altering. When the mindset is positive, it can take you to grand places that were heretofore unimagined.

It is from the positive mindset that we develop an enthusiasm for the progress we are attaining. It is easy to be enthusiastic when our goals and visions become closer and are seen with more clarity. When we actually see that our goals and visions are within our reach, we take on a new level of commitment to making them become a reality.

I have rarely, if ever, seen a winner whine or a whiner win. They don't go together at all! Whiners are traditionally burdened with complacency, negativity, and hopelessness, while winners are focused, enthusiastic, and determined. Who do you think is going to enjoy the best results? It's a no-brainer question and should give us the evidence we need to positively press onward toward our goals and dreams so that we can enjoy the life that we have imagined can come true.

One of the things that has served Donna well in her life is that she is a fanatical reader. I love people who are obsessed with reading good books, as I am as well. It is the simplest, most viable way to learn if we'll just do it. Developing great reading habits is one of the most desirable traits we can internalize if we want to enjoy peace of mind and career progress. Charlie "Tremendous" Jones used to say, "You'll be the same five years from now as you are today except for the people you meet and the books you read!" I concur. If you will become a voracious reader and engender a hunger for knowledge, you will increase the probability of enjoying the fruits of a great life. As for this book, I recommend that you devour it, write in the margins, highlight special parts, and refer to it often. And don't loan this one to anybody. I learned many years ago that loaned books rarely come back. You'll want to refer to this book time and again in the coming years.

Now, let's talk about finances. Many people don't want to worry about them, and they become the people who end up worrying about them the most due to the neglect of the use of sound financial principles. This is a topic where Donna shines, as she has helped innumerable people reach their financial goals by adhering to the practices that she teaches in this book. Some are basic, some are advanced, but all of them are important if we are going to get our financial act in order. Our financial well-being is a measuring stick of the good we have done for ourselves and our family, but also of the service we have rendered to others. As Zig Ziglar used to say, "*You can get anything you want in life if you will just help enough other people get what they want.*"

One noteworthy thing about this book is that the author believes in and respects the differences in people. Indeed, one's individuality is one of their most precious assets. She knows her readers are approaching the reading of this book from many different levels of success and understanding of the topics and principles covered. The uniqueness of her writing style is that she has figured out how to present her financial thesis in a manner that everyone can embrace. It's really quite simple: Follow these principles, and you will advance in your financial quest for progress wherever you are starting from.

Her straightforwardness relating to her own period of failures in her earlier life is admirable. Nobody has experienced a flawless financial life. We have all made mistakes, but it is through that crucible of adversity that we have learned and progressed over time. Many times our failures end up being our springboard to success, as Donna has most adroitly suggested. One of the most valuable inclusions in this book is her premise, touting the importance of having a financial roadmap to follow. Her principles are sound, and her recommendations are well-thought-out.

It is our hope that this book will not only serve as that springboard but also be an inspiration to your development of new habits and solid intentions for building a more rewarding and financially gratifying life. Good luck with the implementation of these ideas in a manner that helps you go to the level to which you aspire.

– Don Hutson

Table of Contents

Introduction

Have you ever found yourself daydreaming about a different life? Maybe you picture yourself traveling the world, starting your own business, or pursuing a passion you've always had. These dreams can seem far-fetched or impossible, but they don't have to be.

The truth is, anyone can pursue their dreams. It takes courage, hard work, and a willingness to take risks, but it is possible to turn those dreams into reality. In this book, we'll explore what it means to go after your dreams and how to overcome the obstacles that stand in your way.

Having a dream means having a vision or a goal that you aspire to achieve in your life. It is something that you deeply desire and are willing to work toward. Dreams can be big or small, personal or professional, short-term or long-term. They give us direction and purpose in life and can motivate us to work harder and overcome obstacles to achieve what we want.

Pursuing your dreams is important because it can bring you happiness, fulfillment, and a sense of accomplishment. When you pursue your dreams, you are more likely to enjoy what you do, and you can find meaning and purpose in your life. It can also lead to personal growth and self-discovery as you learn new things and push yourself to improve.

Moreover, pursuing your dreams can also inspire and motivate others. By following your passions and achieving your goals, you can be a role model and show others that anything is possible if you are willing to work for it and believe in yourself. Your success can inspire others to pursue their own dreams and create a ripple effect of positive change in the world.

Several barriers can prevent people from pursuing their dreams, such as fear of failure, lack of confidence, limited resources, lack of support, and negative self-talk. However, with the right strategies, these barriers can be overcome.

In this book, we will explore how to identify your fears and work through them. You'll learn how to create the roadmap you need to get you to your dreams — and sometimes even faster than you thought possible. We will work on your mindset first because, believe it or not, your mindset is the largest barrier you will have while pursuing your goals. Your mind is a protective mechanism and will stop you to "keep you safe." You're going to learn how to make peace with your mind and show it that there is nothing to be afraid of and that going after your desires is a great thing for you to pursue.

Each chapter has roadmap activities to do in the companion workbook I have created for this book. These are actionable items that will get you closer to your dreams. I have also listed books and other resources that will be valuable to you as you go after everything you want in life.

This book is about setting the proper foundation to pursue your dreams. Creating a proper foundation is essential because it provides the stability, support, and structure necessary to achieve your goals. Without a solid foundation, you may struggle to make progress, encounter obstacles that could have been avoided, or even fail altogether.

A proper foundation can mean different things depending on the specific dream you are pursuing, but some common elements include the following:

- **Clear goals:** Setting specific, measurable, and realistic goals is crucial when pursuing your dreams. A clear understanding of what you want to achieve and how you plan to get there can help you stay focused and motivated.

- **Skill development:** Building the necessary skills and knowledge is essential to achieve your goals. Identify what skills you need to develop and invest time and effort in learning and improving them.

- **Support network:** Surrounding yourself with supportive people who believe in you and your dreams can provide the encouragement and motivation you need when things get tough.

- **Financial stability:** Depending on your dream, it may require financial investment. Ensure you have enough savings, capital or resources to avoid financial stress in pursuing your dreams.

- **Time management:** Proper time management is crucial when pursuing your dreams, as it allows you to maximize your productivity and stay on track with your goals.

Creating a proper foundation for your dreams is vital to success. It enables you to make progress, overcome obstacles, and achieve your goals. By investing in yourself and your foundation, you set yourself up for the best possible chance of success.

It's important to recognize that everyone has some common barriers when pursuing their dreams. I want you to understand right here and now that you are not alone. You are not the only person with fears, lack of resources, lack of confidence, financial constraints, lack of support, or even lack of clarity about what you really want. This book will help you work through these issues and help you get over them.

My name is Donna Connor. I'm a Taurus. I like long walks on the beach… which is a problem since I live in Utah. I'm addicted to *NCIS*, Excel spreadsheets, and pork rinds. I LOVE to travel and go on adventures with my family. I'm a serial entrepreneur. I'm a consummate champion for people going after their dreams. I did college backward — upper division classes in HR management and accounting, then went back to work on my generals years later. I'm still on the eternal college plan of "someday." I may be one of those 90-year-old grandmas who return to school to get that piece of paper. We'll see.

It took me a while, but I realized my clients don't need me to have my college degree. They need my education in the real world of business and finance. Make no mistake — I am educated. I have spent a small fortune on my education outside of a college campus.

My background is in accounting and office administration. I have been in the field for almost 30 years, working for both nonprofit and for-profit companies. I took my mess and got educated. I began to help others by accident and have now been coaching for almost 20 years.

I didn't know what I wanted to be when I grew up until MUCH later in life. My first several businesses were complete and utter failures that took YEARS to pay off the debt I had gotten into with them.

I'm lazy by nature — and felt guilt and shame about it for years — until I recognized that this seemingly negative trait gave me my superpower of creating effective and efficient processes and procedures. I can go into any business and see how to streamline processes to eliminate redundancies and extra work that doesn't need to be done.

I've spent almost 20 years helping couples get out of debt. Almost every single client I have worked with has asked me the same question… "WHY didn't I know this before?!?!" It is a sad state that many people don't learn anything about how to handle money when living at home. Many parents don't know how to handle their money and are too embarrassed to tell us. Many parents thought they were leading by example but never actually sat us down and said, "This is how you balance a checkbook." Schools don't teach it. Well, most don't. I do remember back in the 80s, I went to summer school because they had fun mini-classes you could take, like creative writing and finance. Each subject was a two-week class, and then you would "graduate." One of the classes was how to write a check and balance a checkbook. I laughed that I spent an entire hour for two weeks writing checks and entering them in my checkbook to balance them later, but the skill did me good and I wish more people knew how to do it.

I grew up middle class with a single mom for most of my childhood who worked three jobs just to put food on the table. I grew up thinking that you had to work HARD for your money, and even then, it was iffy if you saw anything worthwhile for your efforts.

I got married young, and we filed for bankruptcy before I was 30. I was mad at my husband at the time because he handled the money, and I had no idea how bad it had gotten until he came home one day and said, "I hired a bankruptcy attorney. Sign here." I was mad for years until I was finally able to recognize he had done the best he could with the skills he had. And I know now there was a certain amount of pride going on as well, and I can only imagine what he felt like when he came home that day to tell me.

Twenty-five years ago, I felt the nudge that I should be doing more with my life, but when I thought about what, I had no idea. I spent about 12 years trying new things, throwing things at the wall to see what would stick, but could not get the traction I needed to make it successful. I kept spinning my wheels, wasting my time and lots of money. Looking back, I can clearly see that I wasn't passionate about anything. I just thought they would make me money, and because I wasn't passionate about it, I wasn't fueled to do the daily work when the excitement wore off. It wasn't until I figured out what I was passionate about that I saw true success in serving my clients, making money, and finding true fulfillment. I learned a lot from those failures, though, and the journey actually led me to where I am now, so I am grateful for it.

My failures are what made me successful. I now own a multi-seven-figure consulting firm. I have a successful coaching and retreat business. I travel multiple times a year with my family. I have created MY Dream Life Plan and want to show you how you, too, can create the life you want without the decades it took me using the proven system I have created to reach your dreams faster with a solid foundation to achieve anything you want. I want to help you to keep going after your dreams when things get hard and barriers are placed in your way — because they will.

You will see throughout this book that I share other books that have made an impact on my life. I am a voracious reader, and while some women are obsessed with buying shoes or purses and such, I buy books. LOTS and LOTS of books. My dream home on my vision board right now is centered around an incredible library that will give me more room for even more books! Even if you dislike reading, I highly recommend you check out the ones I've included here. You don't have to purchase them, you can check them out from your local library. You can also get them on Audible to listen to on your commute each day.

We are all unique. We have different life experiences. We have different likes and interests. We have different values, dreams, and desires. We have different journeys to take. And I LOVE that! Life would be boring if we were all the same.

Whether your dream is big or small, it's never too late to pursue it. This book will be your roadmap to taking that first step toward a life filled with purpose and fulfillment. So, let's begin the journey together and start pursuing your dreams today.

RESOURCES

Go For It! Companion Workbook at

www.go.lifeonpurposeacademy.com/GoForItBookGifts

BOOK RECOMMENDATION

The Go-Giver by Bob Burg

ACTION MAP

1. Download the *Go For It!* Companion Workbook
2. Work through the exercise for this chapter in the *Go For It!* Companion Workbook
3. Start dreaming of the life you want to DESIGN.
4. Read *The Go-Giver*

CHAPTER ONE

Creating YOUR Dream Life Plan

"The purpose of life is a life of purpose."
— Robert Byrne

This week I turn 50. Five-OH! How did I get here? I don't feel 50. I rarely act 50. What does it even mean to act 50? And, of course, those thoughts lead me to wonder, have I lived a successful life? Have I accomplished anything worthwhile? And then, by whose standards am I answering that question?

When I was about 14, I had a darling youth leader in my church in her mid-twenties. She was married and had the cutest little girl. In my eyes, she had an idyllic life. She was pretty, smart, and married to this gorgeous guy, and they had a beautiful home. I wanted to be her when I grew up. She seemed to have it all. I couldn't wait to grow up.

In my mid-twenties, I wondered when I would have my life together like my former youth leader. I wondered when I'd feel as composed as she was at this age. I kept wondering when I'd know what I wanted to do with my life.

In my late twenties, I would divorce and remarry. I still wondered when I would feel as mature and have my life together as my friends I wanted to emulate. I still felt like a teenager. I still felt like I was missing that "one thing" that would make me feel successful. I kept looking forward to the day I would have it together and feel like I had control of my life.

In my mid-thirties, I looked at another friend about 10 years ahead of me in life. She seemed to have life figured out. She had a great career and an awesome family and was always happy. I wanted that. I still couldn't wait to grow up.

Now in my late forties, I've finally figured it out. Hallelujah!

Those ladies I wanted to emulate felt the same way I did. They kept waiting to have their lives figured out. They kept looking at other people to emulate who appeared to have their lives together just as I wanted to emulate them. It's easy to see how much others have accomplished and not recognize what we ourselves have accomplished. Those friends I wanted to emulate felt like they were failing while I was praying I would someday be as awesome as I thought they were.

I will be 50 this week, and I *still* wonder when I will *feel* like an adult. When I will *feel* like I've made it. When I will *feel* like my life has made a difference.

When I stop and look logically at my life, I can see how BLESSED I am! I recognize that I do have my life together. I recognize that I do have that family I wanted when I was 14. I recognize that I do have the career I wanted when I was in my mid-thirties. I recognize that I have designed a life that others are now trying to emulate. I have designed My Dream Life Plan and am now enjoying the fruits of my efforts.

Through this book, I want to show you how to design YOUR dream life and not live by chance. I want to give you permission to dream and go after those dreams. I want to show you how to get past the fears and insecurities you are facing. I want to show you how to work through the steps to live YOUR dream life. I want you to find your passion and make a difference in your life and those around you.

WHAT WE FOCUS ON GROWS

They say that people spend more time planning their vacation than they do planning their lives. I want to change that statistic! Robin S. Sharma said,

"What you focus on grows, what you think about expands, and what you dwell upon determines your destiny." I say if that is the case, then let's focus on what is important and will have a lasting impact on you, and your family.

You may be asking yourself, "What *is* important?"

I can't answer that for you. We all have different paths to take. We all have different purposes and different desires. We have different experiences that have shaped us and will direct our Dream Life Plans. And that's how it should be. That's what makes each and every one unique and fascinating.

I can tell you that for me, making an impact in people's lives is very important to me. I want my life to have meaning and to make a generational difference. As a financial coach, I have been helping couples get out of debt for almost 16 years.

I have been able to teach these couples:

- How to get on the same page with their spouses about money.
- How to get out of debt faster than they ever thought possible.
- How they got themselves in the predicament in the first place to avoid having it happen again — because debt really isn't the issue; it's a symptom of a personal problem.
- How to teach their kids to avoid the same mistakes they made without shame.

As a personal empowerment coach, I have been able to help people through issues they thought they would never be able to overcome. I have been blessed with some incredible trials that have allowed me to have empathy toward people I would not otherwise be able to understand, let alone support and help. I am grateful for the journey I have been on and hope to help others with what I have learned along the way.

When I was younger, I let life happen to me. I didn't know what I wanted to be when I grew up. I didn't have a plan of any kind. I just lived day-to-day. When life changed, I changed with it. I felt like I had no say. It just was what it was.

After my divorce, I started my journey to take control of my life. I wanted to direct my life, not have it directed for me. I started dreaming about everything I ever wanted when I was younger. I started planning to go after those things that were important to me.

All my life I have felt like I was meant for more than the life I was living. I have felt it in my bones that I was meant to do something important. I just had NO FREAKING IDEA what it was. I didn't learn until much later that I could DECIDE what that important thing would be. I didn't recognize that every experience in my life was leading me to figure it out. I didn't see that I was developing skills with my life experiences that would eventually bless others.

Every job, every relationship, even every trial - *especially* every trial — was directing me to my calling.

I am excited to show you how to determine what is important to *you.* I hope as you go through this book and do the exercises in the companion workbook, you will become inspired and motivated to live your life on purpose.

YOUR DREAM LIFE PLAN

I want to show you what an incredible life you can DESIGN. I want to show you how much fun life can be when you set goals and go after them. I want you to be able to DREAM big, GO big, and LIVE big.

- It doesn't matter how much you make — or don't make.
- It doesn't matter how smart you think you are — or aren't.
- It doesn't matter if you have a degree — or not.
- It doesn't matter if you were born with a silver spoon in your mouth — or dirt poor.

YOUR Dream Life Plan takes you from where you are *right now* and guides you through designing your best life possible in complete alignment with your values and desires.

It doesn't matter if you want to make millions or just be able to pay the bills to keep the lights on. We all have different needs and desires – those needs and desires will evolve as well, making it so the journey evolves as you do.

Initially, my Dream Life Plan was simple and designed just to cover my family's basic needs and get out of debt. After we got out of debt, my Dream Life Plan evolved to fully go after my dreams, which I'm now living and loving! I've created and worked on my Dream Life Plan so we are living our lives on purpose. We work hard and play HARDER! My Dream Life Plan now includes adventures around the world.

MY Dream Life Plan is designed to impact people's lives, pay it forward as much as I can, and travel the world. I'm impacting people's lives as I guide them through living their own lives on purpose. My family takes two to three major trips per year. We are making memories with our kids and allowing them to experience things they would never have had an opportunity to do otherwise.

If you notice the word YOUR is emphasized in this chapter's title. It's YOUR Dream Life Plan. This is about YOUR journey. This is about YOUR dreams and desires. We are all individuals and have diverse interests and experiences. There is no one-size-fits-all plan. This is the ultimate "choose your own adventure" plan. You will decide what you want to DO, HAVE, and BECOME in your own life. In the next chapter, you will identify YOUR greatest dreams and desires.

"If you don't know where you're going, any road can get you there."
– Cheshire Cat, Alice in Wonderland

I didn't know where I was going when I was younger, so it didn't matter which road I took. Later though, as I decided where I wanted to go with my life and what I wanted to accomplish, each road mattered very much. I figured out what I wanted to do, have, and become for the rest of my life, and then I needed an accurate map to get me there. Every road I choose either takes me closer to my goals or farther from them. Just like on Google Maps, where we can see all the different routes to get us to the same destination, we can choose which route we want to take on this new journey.

We also get to choose how fast we want to reach our destination. Do we want to take the highway and get there fast, or do we want to take the side roads and go slower?

Perhaps we want to be on the highway but we keep getting detoured. Sometimes life throws us a few detours on our journey. Although I have been frustrated in the moment with the detours I have encountered, I can see now that each was important for my journey. Those detours taught me lessons I needed to learn before I could continue. And sometimes, they got me back on track when I had gotten lost by chasing after shiny objects.

We will all have shiny things that will derail us on our journey. We think they are for our good but are really just distractions keeping us from living our lives on purpose. Learning to decipher which is which will be part of your journey. It took me a long time to recognize how much I chased shiny objects.

I was smart and able to skate through most of high school. I wasn't interested in learning much. I just wanted to hang out with friends, so I did as little as possible while still getting average grades to stay out of trouble. College wasn't on my radar, so I didn't care. It wasn't until I was much older that I learned to love learning. Ironically, I now can't get enough learning. I've read hundreds of books and taken almost as many courses. I feel like I can't get enough input. And though we all know that no learning is ever wasted, there comes a time when you don't need any more input. It's time to overcome our fears and insecurities and start doing the work to get us where we want to go.

Sometimes, our detours may come from loved ones that don't understand our journey and try to stop us. In their mind, they are just trying to protect us from pain, heartache, and failure. However, I have learned that I want challenges. I want to work through them and, eventually, overcome them. It's those challenges that we talk about later on in life. It's those challenges that shape us. It's those challenges that allow us to grow and become better. Do they hurt? Yep. Is it going to be fun going through them? Nope. Are they worth it? ABSOLUTELY! In chapter three, we'll discuss handling those trying to "help" us.

YOUR Dream Life Plan is the ultimate road map to figuring out how to reach your life goals. It identifies:

Where you want to go — what do you want to do, have, and become in this life?

The best route to take — What steps do you need to take to get where you want to go?

The speed limit you set to reach your goals – how fast do you want to reach your goals?

Where to stop to refuel — What do you need to learn to reach your goals? Do you need to go to school, take a course, hire a coach, or simply read a book?

How to find side trips to keep you motivated — learn to celebrate all along your journey!

How to get others to join you on your journey — Who do you want to take with you on this journey and how do you get them cheering you on and working with you to reach your goals?

How to lose the excess baggage that is weighing you down on your journey — Are you in debt? Do you need to work through your fears and anxiety? Do you need to learn to get out of your own way?

What to do once you get to your destination – What can you do now that you have "arrived?" What were the feelings you wanted to feel? What was the purpose of the journey? Now that you're here – what do you want to do, have and become?

How to help others on their journeys – How can you pay it forward? How can you mentor others on their journeys? How do you want to give back?

IDENTIFYING YOUR WHY

A huge part of the plan will be to identify WHY you want to go on this journey in the first place. There WILL be times that you will want to quit. You'll come to a point where the journey may no longer be fun. You'll need to decide whether you want to work through the boredom, pain, and frustrations that hit you in the middle of the journey or if you want to pack your bags and head back home. It will be your WHY that will keep you on the path. It will be your WHY that will keep you motivated. It will be your WHY that will ultimately get you to your destination. We'll delve deeper into identifying your "why" in chapter four.

Let's get started if you're ready to take control of your life, live better than you ever thought possible, and really go after your dreams!

PAIN OF DISCIPLINE VS PAIN OF REGRET

The pain of discipline is the discomfort you feel when making a conscious effort to achieve a goal or maintain a routine. This could be anything from waking up early to exercise, sticking to a strict diet, or working extra hours to achieve a desired outcome. Although it can be challenging and uncomfortable, the pain of discipline is ultimately beneficial in the long run, as it helps us build self-discipline and achieve our goals.

On the other hand, the pain of regret is the feeling of disappointment and remorse that comes from not taking action or making decisions that align with one's values and goals. This can manifest in various ways, such as not pursuing a career opportunity, not speaking up in a difficult situation, or neglecting important relationships. The pain of regret can be especially difficult to bear, as a sense of missed opportunities and what-ifs often accompanies it.

To avoid the pain of regret, it is important to cultivate a sense of self-awareness and prioritize actions that align with your values and goals. This may require making difficult decisions and stepping out of your comfort zone, but it can ultimately lead to a sense of fulfillment and satisfaction in your life.

To overcome the pain of discipline, staying focused on the end goal and finding ways to make the process more enjoyable is important. This could involve finding a workout partner, setting achievable goals, or rewarding oneself for progress made. By embracing the pain of discipline and recognizing its long-term benefits, individuals can achieve personal growth and accomplish their goals.

Being broke is hard. Living within a planned budget is hard. CHOOSE your hard.

Being fat is hard. Living within a defined meal plan and exercise routine is hard. CHOOSE your hard.

Life is about choices. We make them every day. Let's start making choices we won't regret.

BOOK RECOMMENDATION

The Richest Man in Babylon by George S. Clason

ACTION MAP

1. Work through all the exercises for this chapter in the *Go For It!* Companion Workbook
2. Start thinking about the major events in your life and how they have shaped you into the person you are today
3. Read *The Richest Man in Babylon*

CHAPTER TWO

Deciding What You Want to Do, Have and Become

"Thoughts are things, and powerful things at that."

— Napoleon Hill

One of my favorite movies a few years back was Never Been Kissed with Drew Barrymore and Michael Vartan. It's a cute rom-com that I could watch over and over again. The movie's premise was that Drew's character, Josie Geller, was a reporter for the Chicago Sun Times. She was given an opportunity to go undercover back to high school to learn what was important to kids these days. She made friends with a girl named Aldys. During an after-school hangout session, Josie asked Aldys about her hopes and dreams and what she wanted to be when she grew up. Aldys passionately replied, "I want to be a professor of medieval literature, I want to be a novelist, I want to be a weekend flutist, I want to be a potter, I want to be a painter, I want to be an architect, I want to go to Northwestern."

I loved that scene for so many reasons. I felt the same way when I was in high school. There were so many things I *wanted* to do. At the time, I wanted to be a dolphin trainer at SeaWorld, an architect, and a veterinarian. I wanted to create something!

Because money was tight, college was never mentioned in our home. I knew there was no money, and there was no way I felt like I could bring up the subject; I just planned on getting a job and seeing what happened in life. I finally decided to go to our local junior college for one year and could afford it on my own. I took math, English, and an oceanography class. I had no plans. I had no direction. I dropped out and ran off to get married. More on that later…

DREAMING IS GOOD FOR THE SOUL

"All our dreams can come true if we have the courage to pursue them."
— Walt Disney

I have always been a dreamer. I didn't like a lot of things about my life growing up. I dreamed of escape. I dreamt of my dream home, life, family, and what I would do differently in every aspect of my life. It was my escape. And it eventually served me well in life — once I allowed it to do so.

As mentioned in the last chapter, I wandered aimlessly for many years. However, looking back, I can see that there was still some order in my life. I was still being directed, and I love being able to recognize and appreciate the journey I went on back then. Each job I took gave me the skills to move up to the next job. I never realized it was happening, but I became a bookkeeper, and then an accountant. I ended up going to school backward - typical for my life. I had an employer who believed in me and was willing to pay me to go to school and take some accounting classes. I took all my upper-division courses first, and it wasn't until years later that I returned to school for my undergrad work.

I laughed for years about going to school backward, but it helped me recognize and understand that not every journey ends as we thought it would when we started. I am one of those people that loves change. I find it exciting and exhilarating, and I love seeing where I will end up. I'm okay when a plan starts to change; I look for the next pivot and see how much I will learn.

Having an open mind during this journey will make it much more fun and interesting. Starting the journey allows us to open our minds to thoughts and ideas we may not have considered before. If you are open to the possibility that BETTER things are waiting for you in the end, you will be led to be exactly where you need to be and when you need to arrive.

FINDING YOUR VISION IS IMPORTANT FOR YOUR JOURNEY

"Where there is no vision, the people perish..."
— Proverbs 29:18

When I decided to live my life with more purpose and started taking back control of my life, I started reading lots of books on business, mindset, and pretty much anything that I thought would help me understand why I felt called to do something greater with my life. I've read hundreds of books since then. I love "input."

As I started reading books, I was led to start working with coaches and found several mentors over the years who have been instrumental in helping me define my dreams and visions for the future.

The one that started it all for me was *The Power of Starting Something Stupid – How to Crush Fear, Make Dreams Happen, and Live Without Regret* by Richie Norton. That was *the* book that changed my life forever. It was the first book that permitted me to dream and go after my goals with everything I had, with no regrets.

At the time I found and read the book, I had already started my first company. My business partner and I were struggling and frustrated. We were under the misimpression that if we built it, they would come. Yeah, not ONLY NO.... We were up to our eyeballs in debt and no matter what we pivoted to try, nothing was working. We were both frustrated and completely disillusioned with the whole "build your American dream" fantasy.

After reading Richie's book, I reached out to him and told him how much I loved it, how I was sharing it with others, and all that I had learned from it.

He was very gracious, and after some time, we started working with him personally. He helped us tremendously and gave us great advice to try to salvage our sinking ship. Unfortunately, the hole in our ship was too large, and we were too tired from bailing water. We no longer liked, let alone loved, the business enough to fight for it. We cut our losses and eventually shut it down.

But here's the thing. I learned more from that "failing" business than I ever did from my later successful ones. It's from that failure that I base my decisions today. From those lessons, I strive for better outcomes and am better at what I do. Don't EVER let fear of failure stop you. Don't ever let actual failure stop you. It's not failing if you learn from it and become better from it. It wasn't a failure, it was a lesson. And an important lesson at that. Sometimes those lessons hurt in a big way, but they will always be beneficial if you allow them to be.

Working with Richie through that one business helped me define exactly what I wanted to do with my life, find my passion, and to figure out what I needed to do so I wouldn't have regrets later in life for not going after my dreams with everything I had.

That is what I want this book to be for you. I want to give you permission to dream, and I mean *really* DREAM. I want you to be able to turn that dream into a VISION that will guide you to designing YOUR Dream Life Plan. I want to help you identify your fears and teach you how to overcome them. I want to help you streamline the process to arrive at your destination faster than you thought possible while still learning the skills you need to build a solid foundation for success. I want to help you see that NOW is the time to start.

WHAT DO YOU WANT TO DO, HAVE, AND BECOME?

This is where the fun starts!!! This is where I want you to play full-out. I want you to throw off your limiting beliefs – you know the ones – what will people think? Who am I to do this? What experience/knowledge do I have to do this?

STOP THOSE LIMITING THOUGHTS RIGHT NOW!

We're going to go through an exercise to remove those limiting beliefs later on, but for right now, I want you to dream as if nothing is stopping you... because the truth is (as you'll later learn), there is NOTHING stopping you... except yourself.

This exercise is the beginning of designing YOUR Dream Life Plan! As mentioned before, it doesn't matter which road you take if you don't know where you're going. This is where you DECIDE where you want to go. This is where you get to put down on paper everything that is in your head and in your heart.

When people are asked to make a list like this, they usually only come up with two or three things. If pushed, they can come up with five to seven things. Here is what I want from you. I want 50, yes 50, things on your list! I want you to really dig deep. I want you to take your time. I want you to ponder and pray if you are the praying type. I want this list to keep growing over the next few days and weeks. I want you to dream BIG! I want pie-in-the-sky, pipe dream, fantasy items on your list. I want you to be laughing out loud, saying 'Yeah, right!!" as you add items to your list. No, I haven't lost my mind. There is a purpose for this. There is something exhilarating about thinking "what if" with no limitations.

It's time to start dreaming! I only have a few lines in the book. This is where I want you to put your top five things in each category. Use the *Go For It! Companion Workbook* for this exercise. Keep it with you. Add to it as thoughts come to you. Don't discount any thoughts that come. There is a reason you have them. It doesn't mean you have to act on them, but there is a purpose to having them on the list.

What are the top five things you want to **DO** in life?

1.
2.
3.
4.
5.

What are the top five things you want to **HAVE** in life?

1.
2.
3.
4.
5.

What are the top five things you want to **BECOME** in life?

1.
2.
3.
4.
5.

How did that feel?!? How fun was that for you? Did you feel reluctant? Did you do it anyway?

We're going to do another exercise right now that will change *everything* for you. We're going to break the limiting beliefs you felt during this exercise, and we're going to fight the fears that came up.

If you really do the work coming up, there will be nothing that stops you on your journey to design the life you want! I want you to play full out. This part can be uncomfortable, but it will break the chains holding you back if you do it.

Use the Go For It! Companion Workbook to complete this assignment. The space here is for your top answers and the ones you really want to work through to remove the roadblocks on your journey.

What came up for you during that exercise? List the good, the bad, and the ugly.

1.
2.
3.

What fears or limiting beliefs came up while you worked on that?

1.

2.

3.

Whose voice came up saying you can't do these things? We all have them. It's okay. Who are the people you are most afraid of that will judge you for taking this journey?

1.

2.

3.

This exercise may have been hard. It may have been hard to admit to things you knew, but didn't want to acknowledge. I'm proud of you. I've been right here where you are. I can promise you that identifying these things will make your journey easier. When you know what you are up against, you can plan for it and make plans ahead of time.

LIMITING BELIEFS

Limiting beliefs are negative, self-sabotaging thoughts that hold us back from achieving our goals and fulfilling our potential. They are beliefs we hold about ourselves, others, or the world around us that limit us somehow. These beliefs can be based on past experiences, cultural conditioning, or simply the stories we tell ourselves.

Examples of limiting beliefs include thoughts like "I'm not good enough," "I'm too old to start something new," or "I'll never be successful." These beliefs can be so deeply ingrained in our minds that we may not even be aware of them, but they have a profound impact on our lives and the decisions we make.

One of the biggest problems with limiting beliefs is that they create a self-fulfilling prophecy. When we believe that we can't achieve something, we are less likely to try, and if we do try, we are more likely to give up when things get tough. This can lead to a cycle of negativity and failure that reinforces the belief and makes it even harder to break free.

The good news is that limiting beliefs can be overcome with awareness and effort. The first step is to identify the beliefs that are holding you back. This can be done through introspection and reflection or by working with a therapist or coach who can help uncover these beliefs.

Once you have identified your limiting beliefs, you can begin to challenge them. Ask yourself questions like "Is this belief really true?" or "What evidence do I have to support this belief?" Often, you will find that your beliefs are based on assumptions or generalizations that are not necessarily true.

Another way to challenge limiting beliefs is to look for counterexamples. If you believe you are not good enough, for example, try to identify times in your life when you have succeeded or accomplished something you are proud of. This can help to shift your perspective and build confidence in your abilities.

It's important to replace limiting beliefs with more positive, empowering ones. This can be done through affirmations, visualization, or simply focusing on the positive aspects of your life and your abilities. The more you reinforce positive beliefs, the more they will become ingrained in your mind and the more likely you are to achieve your goals.

Limiting beliefs can be a major obstacle to success and fulfillment, but they can be overcome with awareness and effort. By identifying and challenging these beliefs, we can break free from the cycle of negativity and self-sabotage and create a more positive, empowering narrative.

Do the exercises in the *Go For It!* Companion Workbook to work through the limiting beliefs you are experiencing right now. You can come back to the exercise again with additional limiting beliefs that come up on your journey because they will come up. As you get to new levels of success, new devils of beliefs will come up for you.

Now it's time to list everything that could stop YOU on this journey. If we were on a real road trip, those items would be getting a flat tire, running out of gas, the radiator overheating, etc. So, we would want to make sure we had a spare tire in the car, we would want to make sure we are watching the fuel gauge and stopping to refuel when necessary, and we might want to make sure we have an extra gallon of water in the car.

In this real-life journey, we want to identify the things that can stop you or detour you and plan ahead of time how you will overcome those issues NOW so that you can get back on the road again as fast as possible. Some issues that come to mind are stress, lack of sleep, fear, chasing shiny objects that take you off the road you are on, etc. Ways to combat these issues might be organizing your time, prioritizing your work, getting to bed on time, and working through the fear you may be feeling by journaling or other exercises we'll review in another chapter. The big one will be staying focused and keeping your eyes on the road. You will have to ask yourself repeatedly on this journey, will this get me closer to my destination or farther?

Issues I may experience:

1.

2.

3.

Solutions for those issues:

1.

2.

3.

There are a lot of famous people and companies out there that we only see the end result of—the glory, if you will. You don't see the setbacks, the time, energy, sweat, and tears. It took Dyson five years and 5,127 prototypes before they created the first bagless vacuum. Edison is quoted as saying, "I have not failed. I have just found 9,999 ways that do not work." There will be struggles. Fear will creep in. People will doubt you. You will doubt yourself. And that is okay. It's normal. It's also a test to see how badly you want your dreams. George Addair is quoted as saying, "Everything you want is on the other side of fear." This is why it is so important to figure out exactly what you want and how to overcome the obstacles that will get in your way.

CREATING THE ROADMAP

"Nurturing and Living your dream is the most thrilling adventure of life."
- Invajy

Now that you've identified your top five things you want to DO, HAVE, & BECOME, what do we do with that information? Now it's time to act upon it! Out of the top 15 ideas, which one speaks to you? Which one is screaming in your head, *Pick me!* If none of them are, then you need to go back to the workbook and reevaluate which one to work on. You may have all five screaming, *Pick me!* and that's okay as well. We're just going to focus on one because keeping your focus on one at a time will allow you to arrive at your destination quicker. Once you do "arrive," you can focus on the next item on the list. Then it's just wash, rinse, and repeat for everything you want to DO, HAVE, & BECOME.

You may look at your list and realize that there is a theme to the items on your list. You may also notice that it makes sense to go after your dreams in a certain order. That's perfect.

So now that you have the ONE thing you're going to focus on right now, it's time to start building out your road map for this journey.

Make a list of what it would take to make this one thing come to fruition. Do you need to read a book? Find a coach/mentor? Attend a training session? Get a degree? Make a list of every option or task you think needs to happen to reach your destination in the Go For It! Companion Workbook.

Let's say you want to start a photography business…

You'd need to follow these steps:

1. Decide what types of photography services you'll offer.
2. Take classes if you need them.
3. Develop your business plan.
4. Decide your business structure.

5. Create a business name.
6. Officially establish your business.
7. Purchase needed equipment and supplies.
8. Create marketing materials.
9. Market, market, market.

...or you wanted to become an Architect.
You'd need to follow these steps:

1. Earn your bachelor's degree in architecture.
2. Participate in an internship program.
3. Become licensed.
4. Apply for an architect position.
5. Earn professional certifications.
6. Consider a master's degree.

...or you wanted to become a professional singer.
You'd need to follow these steps:

1. Pick a Niche. Becoming a professional singer requires strong vocals, thick skin, and the persistence to succeed.
2. Find a Unique Angle. The singing market is saturated.
3. Perfect your Voice.
4. Understand the Industry.
5. Record Something.
6. Book Some Shows.
7. Get Online.
8. Network.

These are broad steps to reach for each of these samples. Under each of those major steps, there are smaller steps that you need to take as well. Let's say you want to become an architect. Step one is to get a degree. Simple enough, right? Well, what schools are you going to apply to? What scholarships can you earn? Where are you going to live while you're in school?

This may seem daunting, but it is actually very powerful to outline what needs to be done and then just take it ONE. STEP. AT. A. TIME. You have your road map. You know what you need to do, so just do it!

Whatever it is YOU want to Do, Have, and Become has steps that you need to accomplish to reach your destination. What are they for your first goal? Use the Go For It! Companion Workbook to start your roadmap.

Most likely, someone else has done exactly, or at least similarly, what you want to do. Who has accomplished what you want to accomplish? How did they do it? How can you improve upon what they did? What can you learn from their journey?

READY, SET, ACTION!

"Don't let the fear of striking out hold you back."
— Babe Ruth

If you've done the work in the companion book, you've identified your first destination on your journey and the steps necessary to reach that destination. Now it's time to take ACTION!! It's time to hop in the car and begin this journey!

What are you going to do first, and when are you going to do it? Make this plan REAL. Add your steps and set a date for each step in your plan. Remember, a goal without a plan is just a wish. Make the plan! Do the Work! See the Success!

Don't worry about missing steps or having too many steps. Just take it ONE step at a time. Breathe. Have faith. Don't get overwhelmed with everything you need to do. If you are moving forward and taking action, the next step will reveal itself at the right time. A great question to ask yourself after taking each action step is, "What did I learn from completing this action?" What action step do I need to take next? Your action steps may change throughout the course of the journey as you get better at knowing what to do and learning from your actions.

CELEBRATE!

You need to celebrate along your journey. Especially if what you want will take time to achieve. Waiting until the end is hard. You can burn out if you aren't celebrating wins along the way. Find ways to celebrate KEY milestones. If you are losing weight, I'd say celebrate every five pounds and do something nice for yourself. Get a manicure, buy new clothes, and get a massage. You know best what motivates you to work hard when the luster of the journey has worn off a bit.

Use the Go For It! Companion Workbook to make your complete list of celebration points and what your reward will be for each achievement.

BOOK RECOMMENDATIONS

The Power of Starting Something Stupid by Richie Norton

ACTION MAP

1. Work through all the exercises for this chapter in the *Go For It!* Companion Workbook
2. Achieving massive goals is never a walk in the park. Those who push forward get rewarded. Consider listing five things you must do today that may be uncomfortable but will get you a few steps closer to your Dream Life.
3. Read *The Power of Starting Something Stupid.*

CHAPTER THREE

Including Others to Achieve Your Dreams & Goals

"Life is better with friends!"

- Unknown

Road trips are better with family and friends. It's fun to plan and prepare for the trip, but the real adventure is being on the road. And being with friends and family is much better than being alone. It's playing music or listening to books. It's about the car games and the talks. It's about the snacks and stops and what you get to see out the windows. It's about making memories.

YOUR Dream Life Plan is the same as a road trip. You've planned and you've prepared and now you're deciding who you are bringing along with you for the journey. I hope your family is in the car with you. I hope you are able to bring some close friends with you. I hope you get to meet some amazing friends along your journey that will hop in and join you along the way as well.

I love road trips. And I mean LOVE. I love everything about them. We have family who are 17 hours away and we go a couple of times a year to see them. I love those trips. I love driving. I love the time to listen and talk and think. When I was in high school, my best friend and I wanted to become long-haul truck drivers so we could see the country. LOL. I laugh at that idea for two reasons. One, I didn't realize until later that we'd only see the highways with no side trips to beautiful places. And two, I can barely get my minivan into a parking stall straight half the time, I can't even imagine parking a truck and 70-foot trailer. Ridiculous.

We are on the road a LOT. We have been blessed that we've only had a few issues in all the years we have traveled. I've hit deer multiple times. The worst one was on our way to Colorado from Utah. My husband had flown out to help his parents clean up the family land because they were going to sell it after living there for 40 years. My husband had been out there a week working and I was driving out alone with two of my kids in the middle of the night.

I was on I-70 and just going through Green River, Utah. I-70 is a divided highway in that section. There were two lanes eastbound, and I was just getting ready to pass a slow-moving semi on the left when I saw the deer on the side of the road. You don't have to worry about deer if they have their head down and are eating, but you do if they are looking around. Unfortunately, this deer was looking around and then straight at our headlights. The speed limit on that stretch of highway is 80 miles per hour. And just as I was edging out the semi, that darn deer tried to run across the highway. He evaded the semi, but there was nothing I could do, and I hit him straight on. That deer had almost made it because all the damage was on the driver's side.

THANKFULLY, someone had recently told me to NEVER swerve for animals. They told me that swerving almost inevitably makes it worse — as in you losing control of your vehicle, hitting other vehicles, etc.

My van was toast. That semi kept driving, but I was down. I was in between the two exits of Green River in the middle of the night, alone with two scared kids. When I pulled over to the side of the road, I realized a couple of things. First, I couldn't turn very well. Second, once parked, I realized I couldn't open my door. I was now scared too, thinking that the deer was still attached to my car. I couldn't see anything from where I was, so I had to have my daughter get out and look for what was blocking my door. Again, thankfully, there was no deer. Phew!

When we hit the deer, it jammed the front panel of my van back into the door, which was why I couldn't open it. It also affected the wheel well and wouldn't let the tire turn without scraping it.

I immediately called my husband to tell him what happened. I knew we had roadside assistance but couldn't find the information in the glove box. He was concerned about us being stranded on a dark highway. He was going to get roadside assistance set up for me. In the meantime, I climbed over the center console and got out of the van to assess the full damage. It was pretty bad, but I think I could have made it to Colorado if it hadn't been for the wheel well.

I called 911 and told them where we were. A few minutes later, a highway patrol trooper arrived to help. I told him about the deer, and he went to look for it. A minute later, we heard a gunshot. The deer had been suffering. He also asked me to walk down the road with him. As I did, he told me how glad he was that I hadn't swerved to avoid hitting the deer. He showed me that at the point of contact, there was a significant drop-off into the median. I would have surely rolled my van at that speed and there is no way of knowing if we would have survived. WOW! That was sobering!

The patrolman told me that there was a hotel in town and a mechanic could look at my car in the morning. A few minutes later my husband called and told me that assistance wasn't on the way. He was livid! I hadn't seen him that upset in a very long time. Apparently, we had roadside assistance, but only during regular business hours. Say what?!!? So here he is hundreds of miles away with his wife and kids with a disabled vehicle broken down on the side of the road in the middle of the night. I reassured him we were fine, that we had the patrolman with us still and that he'd follow us back into town to make sure we made it to the hotel.

The next morning, I opened the passenger door, climbed over the center console, and drove to the mechanic. I sat there in front of their big shop window and realized I'd have to climb out over that center console again with everyone in the shop watching me. Heavy sigh. Long story short, they wanted

WAY too much, I'd be stuck in Green River for a week waiting for parts, etc. They were kind enough to help me get my bumper back on my van and hammer out some of the wheel well so I could drive it. In the meantime, my husband found another mechanic in Grand Junction who would work with our insurance. Since Grand Junction is a larger town, they also had a place I could rent a car so we could continue on our trip to Pueblo, Colorado. Carefully, I drove from Green River, Utah to Grand Junction, Colorado, which was 102 miles away. Our van was full, and they didn't have a van to rent, so we had to cram a LOT of stuff into a midsize sedan. But we made it to Pueblo that day! We had a great time with the family. We were able to help them with cleaning up and organizing and found out our van would be fixed in time for our planned trip home. Yay!

The point of this story is that I could have made all those arrangements on my own. It would have taken a lot of time and delayed me significantly more, but I could have done it. Thankfully, I didn't have to. My husband was my support team and did most of the legwork so I could be present with my kids, who were very scared. We not only want to have supportive people with us in our car on this journey, but we want supportive people on the sidelines cheering us on and helping us when we need it.

It's time to identify who YOU want on this journey with you, whether it is in the car or on the sidelines. It's also important to recognize and prepare for times that people will be in the car with you and other times when they will be on the sidelines. There is never a wrong time for them to be in certain places. You just need to recognize the timing and understand that it's okay.

- It doesn't matter who you want to join you on your journey, the process is the same.
- Tell them your dream.
- Invite them to dream with you.
- Identify what's in it for them when they get on board.
- Invite them to sit in a specific seat in your dream.
- Allow them to work on your dream with you.

- Reciprocate! Allow them to dream as well. Let them share their dreams. Support them the way you want to be supported. Work together on their dreams. Celebrate their wins together.

The clearer you can be in explaining your dreams, the more likely they will hop on board. You need to show the value of what you are trying to accomplish. Show them your entire vision to not only see what you want to do right now but how you see it growing in the future. Be very clear on what your dream means to you and to them.

To get their buy-in, you need to let them have a say in your dream. Let them participate in dreaming about it, growing it, and defining it. Let them work with you to sketch it out. Allow them the space to both support you and express their concerns. The more conversation you have upfront, the more likely they will stay on board with you for the entire journey.

We are sometimes misguided into thinking that if we don't do something on our own, we can't experience the glory of accomplishing it. That is the farthest thing from the truth! Look at many sports. It takes teamwork. It takes a pit crew. It takes coaches. Very few people truly accomplish great things on their own. They do get the glory, but there is a whole team behind them that helped them along the way. Don't let pride keep you from including others on your journey to help you.

They need to have a clear understanding of how you see them fitting in on your journey and how they play a part in it. Don't ever make them feel like they can't be a part of it. Make sure they get to play a part they want to play. Ask them where they want to sit for the ride.

- Allow them to work on your dream with you.
- Set interim goals you want to arrive at.
- Identify how you'll know that you've arrived at each destination.
- Celebrate your arrival together!
- Let the journey be fun.
- Reciprocate!

While getting people on board is the same, there are reasons certain people may not be as willing to support you and your dreams as you hoped they would. Let's talk about some of the reasons they might not be as willing to join you on your journey as you would like — there may be some people who don't want you to take the journey at all — and how to handle each situation.

Our Spouses:

Sometimes our spouses will be eager to get on board and ride with us on our journey. That is a great time! The music is playing, and you're having great talks, and making incredible memories. Other times, you have to work extra hard to convince them to even let you take the journey in the first place, let alone get them to join you. So let's identify and talk about some of their concerns and how to overcome them. The obvious ones are time, money, and fear.

Time. There are only so many hours in the day. We are already stretched thin with so many things on our plate. Our spouses are trying to understand how you are going to fit in one more thing, let alone a big thing like your dream, and still find time for them. Working together to make time for your dream goes a long way. As I told my husband that I wanted to write this book, he rolled his eyes and asked when was I going to find the time to add one more thing?

My running joke has always been that my plate is never full because I can just run over to IKEA and buy a bigger plate. Between being a wife, a mother to two very active teenagers still at home, a general manager, a financial advisor, and running another business, I might be able to see where he might wonder how I was going to fit in writing a book! To be honest, I was even wondering about that. My daughter is in color guard and working, while my son is in lacrosse and a bowling league. We have things going several nights per week and on Saturdays.

I told my husband that while the kids are either working or at practice Monday through Thursday and he was busy with softball, golf or bowling as well, I'd work hard Monday through Thursday nights and make sure I was available to the family Friday nights and Saturdays and Sundays. It seemed like a great plan. But I found myself feeling the "mom guilt" on the nights the kids were home and upstairs while I was holed up in the basement writing or working. I also had SERIOUS FOMO going on. I was jealous that they were upstairs laughing and joking and enjoying life while I was holed up in the basement writing or working. I found myself wandering upstairs all the time, trying to be a part of the activities. I wanted to laugh and joke and not work so hard. Sound familiar? I wanted this dream, but he didn't. I was doing this to myself.

After several weeks of making no progress, I talked to one of my coaches about the situation and told her that I needed to change things up. I'm a morning person, and by that I mean I have no problem waking up early and I'm actually way more productive in the first few hours of the day than I am the entire rest of the day. When I worked in an office, I asked to change my hours from seven to four instead of the regular eight to five. I got more done in that one hour of quiet time than I usually got done the rest of the day. I took my cue from that experience. I now get up at five a.m. and write for two hours while my kids and husband are asleep. It's perfect! I'm up, I'm productive, I'm not missing out on anything, and I don't feel any guilt while everyone is asleep. I've gotten more done in the past two weeks than I did the entire first month. I'm now available every night and get to spend time with my family. I'm accomplishing what I want without sacrificing time with my family.

You're going to need to find what works best for your situation. You'll also need to be flexible if it isn't working and try different things until you find what works.

Money. This is a big one for most spouses. What is your dream going to cost the family? Where are you going to get the money from? How much debt are you going to rack up? What if it doesn't work? Doesn't feel very supportive, does it? Unfortunately, for us dreamers, these are the reality checks to our dreams. They are valid points. They are necessary discussions to have and to work through. You need to be on the same page with your spouse. You need to figure these things out and get their support or it will be an uphill battle the entire time.

Though money issues are hard conversations, there are productive ways to have them that don't wind up in a fight every single time.

Fear. Our spouses may not admit it, but they are afraid that if you go after your dreams, they won't have a place in your new life. They are afraid that you will go on your journey and never come back. It will be your job to help them see that you want them to come on the journey with you and that you don't plan on leaving them behind.

When I was dreaming of starting a farm and creating a place for veterans to work and grow, I knew with every fiber of my being that my husband had no interest in farming. I knew that my dream wasn't his dream. He was out of work at the time, and I was dreaming of this HUGE Disneyland dream where I could see every aspect of what would be included on the land, who would manage it, who would benefit from it, etc. He couldn't see it. He hadn't spent months researching it, designing it, and dreaming it as I had. He only knew what I could articulate.

One day we were out for a walk, and he finally asked me where I saw him in this dream of mine. I was honest with him and told him that I hadn't included him in my dream because I knew he didn't want to do anything that would be required to run it. I could tell that hurt him. I explained that I wasn't going to force him to do something he didn't want to do. He appreciated that. We started talking about everything I saw that needed to be done and he talked about which parts he'd be interested in helping with and which ones he wouldn't. Once he could see himself in my vision, he was more on board. The timing wasn't right to go after this dream, but I still have it in the back of my mind. I still have the business plan. Who knows if I will ever pursue it. But this experience taught me the importance of including my husband, allowing him to dream with me and allowing him to decide how involved he wanted to be in my dream.

Unfortunately, not everyone has a spouse that will be as supportive as we want them to be. Sometimes, we have to allow them their space and understand, or at least try to understand, why they don't want to be in the car with you. As much as we want them to be in the car with us, we need to be supportive of them whether they want to be in the car or not. It can be a difficult road to navigate. It can add stress to our relationships. It can lead us to be on parallel paths.

You have to navigate it through. You can't ignore it. You can't hide from it. You have to face it. Sometimes, it is your spouse that will be the greatest challenge for you on your journey, but you will learn a lot from the situation. You will learn how much you want your dream. You will learn how to make your dream clearer for others to understand better. You will learn how to navigate negative people. You will learn how to create space for others as you want space for yourself.

And, in the hardest situations, you may even need to choose between your dream and your spouse. Those are rare and extreme cases. And, in no way am I encouraging you to choose your dream over your spouse, but sadly, people have had to make those choices.

It's called authenticity vs attachment. Dr. Gabor Maté has studied this dynamic for years. He says, "People have two needs: attachment and authenticity. When authenticity threatens attachment, attachment trumps authenticity." He explains that as children, we learn to sacrifice authenticity for connection. Dr. Maté says it's done mostly unconsciously and that our body's intelligence recognizes that if we are our full, vibrant selves, we'll lose the attachment with our parents. He goes on to say that humans are wired for attachment like all mammals and will do whatever it takes to experience it. I highly recommend listening to the video. The link is at the end of the chapter.

Our Children:

Children are easier to convince to join you on your journey. As Dr. Maté explains, we all want to experience attachment. You going after your dreams opens the door for them to dream about what they want and for them to go after their dreams. I hope you show them how to be authentic and support them to find their authentic selves. I hope you are holding space for them to explore, try new things, and pursue what they are passionate about. The more you allow them to do so, the more they are willing to allow you to go after your dreams.

Just as you did for your spouse, you need to be clear about your dream with your children. You need to include them in dreaming and planning. You need to show them what's in it for them. You need to work with them to figure out where they fall into the dream and what they can do to help you accomplish it.

To children love is spelled T. I. M. E. Doing anything worthwhile takes effort. Finding ways to make sure you're still available for your children will be important. Working while they are taking a nap, at school, at work, etc. will allow you to get things done uninterrupted and prevent them from resenting your absence. As I mentioned above in my story, I was experiencing FOMO and guilt, they were resenting everything that was preventing me from being with them. When I made the change to work in the morning, it allowed me to have more time with them and let them know that I'm available to them when they need me. Does that mean I don't ever work when they are home and available? No. It just means that I am more conscious about how I spend my time.

Children are the ultimate accountability partners too! I can't tell you how many times my kids have held me accountable. Because we have discussed what it will take to reach my dreams, they know when I should be writing or doing other work. They know when I shouldn't be spending money. They know when I should be doing any number of things, and they have NO problem reminding me that I should or should not be doing something. They love having that power. It's funny to hear them put me in my place. They have taught me a lot and helped me find a nicer way to remind them to do things as well. We have mutual respect for each other. It's been an incredible experience to include my children.

Our Extended Family and Friends:

Bless their hearts! They only want what's best for us – at least what they deem is best for us. They are only trying to protect us. They think they are doing the right thing. You will have to become strong, know your value, be clear about your dream, and be prepared to just "smile and wave."

Sometimes you can convince them, but most of the time you can't. All you can do is follow your own path. It isn't theirs to be on. It isn't theirs to understand. It isn't theirs to judge, but we all know there is that one (or many) that will. Just own your journey. Live your journey. If they can support you, let them in, and if they can't, just know that it is their issue, not yours to fix.

There is a meme that says, "No one is supposed to understand your calling. It wasn't a conference call." People may not understand what it is we feel called to do. That's okay. Show them grace.

We all want certain people to come on this journey with us. All we can do is explain the dream, show them what is in it for them, invite them to come along, and then hold space for them regardless of their decision.

We talked about inviting the people we care about to come along on our journey, but don't forget about the people you haven't even thought of yet. You'll need to be open and know that as you start this journey, you will be led to people who will be able to open doors for you that you haven't even recognized need to be opened yet. You'll find people who can get you the resources you need. It's an amazing phenomenon. Make sure your eyes are open. You will receive inspiration, direction, and resources from sources known and unknown.

RESOURCES

Video: Authenticity vs Attachment by Dr. Gabor Maté

BOOK RECOMMENDATIONS

How to Win Friends and Influence People by Dale Carnegie

Crucial Conversations: Tools for Talking When Stakes are High by Kerry Patterson

ACTION MAP

1. Work through all the exercises for this chapter in the *Go For It!* Companion Workbook.

2. Watch the video *Authenticity vs Attachment* by Dr. Gabor Mate.
3. Read *How to Win Friends and Influence People.*
4. Read *Crucial Conversations: Tools for Talking When Stakes are High.*
5. Start having discussions with the people you want on your journey. Explain your dream. Show them what's in it for them. Show them how you see them helping you. Find out if they are interested in being in that role or if they have a better idea of how they can help you reach your goals.

CHAPTER FOUR

The Secrets to reaching Your Goals FASTER

"Quality questions create a quality life. Successful people ask better questions, and as a result, they get better answers"

– Tony Robbins

This topic is one of my favorites. As I mentioned in the introduction, I've been helping couples get out of debt for almost 20 years. I actually worked with one couple three times to get out of debt! I spent months working with them to get out of debt. They were THRILLED and cried and couldn't believe the day had finally come. They went off on their own and about six months later they called me in total shame because they were back in debt again. So, we started working together and got them out of debt again. Again, they went off on their own. Again, they reached out about nine months later. Again, they were in debt. I was perplexed, to say the least. I was thinking, "What is wrong? They have the skillset. I've taught it to them three times!" It was then that I realized that 90 percent of YOUR Dream Life Plan journey is about mindset, not skillset. Mindset is the game-changer. Mindset is what helps us win or lose. It's that six inches between our ears that will try to stop us over and over from going after our dreams. Our mindset is what helps us get over the hurdles when everything seems to be crashing down on us. Our mindset is what helps us get past that wall that we keep hitting over and over again. Our brain is meant to protect us, and it will try over and over again.

If you can master your mindset, you can master ANYTHING!

When you're on the road to your journey, nothing matters if your engine isn't working properly. It doesn't matter if you have a full tank if your engine needs work. Your mindset is the engine of your journey to Design YOUR Dream Life Plan.

That is why the first section of this book is all about mindset. I'll be honest. My 15-year-old son can teach you about going after your dreams and creating a budget and several other skill sets I teach you in this book. He's been taught and he's actively using the skills you're going to learn by reading this book.

We need to recognize that our brains were designed to solve problems. We need to allow it to do its job. We find ourselves stuck sometimes and we need to learn to ask ourselves the right questions in the right order to solve the problems we are facing. If we can learn to ask better questions, we will get better answers.

When we start dreaming of what we want to DO, HAVE, and BECOME, our brain immediately asks, "How?" How are we going to get that? How are we going to do that? How are we going to become that? And the minute we ask ourselves "how," our brains shut down. It goes into protective mode and will start to tell you all the reasons why it won't work. It goes into all the lies we've been fed about not being good enough, smart enough, or educated enough. It's a metaphoric tire boot that prevents you from moving on your journey. It holds you in place — fearful, frustrated, and forlorn.

There is a formula that if you master, will allow you to reach all your dreams FASTER than you ever thought possible. This shortcut will get your brain working *for* you instead of *against* you. It will become your greatest advocate and problem solver instead of trying to stop you at every turn. So, let's get your brain doing what it's meant to do to help you on your journey. This is where you learn to start asking better questions!

You need to stop your brain from first asking how and to implement this formula to get better results.

Question 1: What do I want?

Question 2: Why do I and my family want it?

Question 3: Who benefits from this?

Question 4: When can I get this done?

Question 5: Where can I do this?

Question 6: What am I willing to sacrifice to accomplish this?

Question 7: How can I do this?

Can you see how changing the order of the questions allows your brain to go into hyperdrive to help you figure things out? By asking these questions in this order, you've already eliminated your brain's natural objections! You've taken your brain out of protection mode. It can now see the value of your dream and will start problem-solving for you! How awesome is that?!

Let's go through this process with a real-life example. Let's say you want to save $20,000 to start a business. Normally, your brain would naturally ask itself how and come up with 20 reasons you can't do it. You don't make enough. You've never had that much money before. You need the money for other things. You're not smart enough to find ways to earn it. And the list goes on and on.

So, now let's change the order of the questions and see where it gets us. Let's say you want to save $20,000 and start a consulting firm. Let's see how changing the order of the questions you ask changes your outcome.

What do I want?

I want to start a consulting firm that will save companies money on their copiers and printers and put contracts in their favor instead of the vendor's favor. My consulting firm will allow companies to save a lot of time and money. It will add to the company's overall bottom line and create a more financially sound company for its owners and employees.

Why do I and my family want this?

My consulting firm will make a difference in businesses and individual lives. Knowing that I am making a difference to stabilize companies legally and financially, makes me proud and will allow me to feel good about what I do. Knowing that my company only takes a percentage of the cost savings we create, makes good financial sense that will provide a good living for my employees as well as my family. Knowing that I can run my business from anywhere thanks to great technology, affords my family to live a lifestyle we only dreamt of possible.

Who benefits from this?

My clients, whom we help by contributing to their bottom line and putting contracts in their favor.

My client's employees, who are now working for a financially stronger company.

My employees, who can make a difference with what they do and the money they earn.

My family, who get to see me more and can pay our bills and have a great life with what I earn.

My friends, whom I can serve more and help more with money my business generates.

My community, who I can support and give back to on a regular basis.

Phew! That's a lot of positive reinforcement for our brains to consider!

When can I get this done?

Well, if we take $500 per paycheck and put it into savings, that will take 20 months. If we also throw extra money at the dream, we can get there faster. If we take our tax returns for both years and add it to the savings account, that will save us six months, so now we can have this done in 14 months!

Once I have the money, I can start working on this part-time until the business has a couple of clients closed. Then I could quit my job and go full-time in the business.

Where can I do this?

I can be working full time while we are in saving mode. I can then run the business from home or on the road. All I need is a good internet connection and a quiet place to make calls. Making my company a virtual office where all my employees can do their jobs from home keeps overhead low and offers a great benefit to my employees. It means I can travel with my family and still keep working.

What am I willing to sacrifice to accomplish this?

I'm willing to give up some sleep now in order to put hours in before the kids wake up to move towards this goal without sacrificing time with my family. I'm willing to go out to eat less and not add to my wardrobe this year in order to put more money away to go out on my own sooner.

Now, we get to ask ourselves the BIG question…

How can I do this?

We've taken all the objections out and allowed our brains to start working on more answers for us! Now is the time to be patient and have faith. Your brain will surprise you as you will have ideas come to you on how to accomplish this great goal you've set out to accomplish.

DIVING DEEPER INTO IDENTIFYING YOUR WHY

A huge part of the plan will be to identify WHY you want to go on this journey in the first place. There WILL be times that you will want to quit. You'll come to a point where the journey may not be fun anymore. You'll need to decide whether you want to work through the boredom, pain, and frustrations that hit you in the middle of the journey or if you want to pack your bags and head back home. It will be your WHY that will keep you on the path. It will be your WHY that will keep you motivated. It will be your WHY that will ultimately get you to your destination. We'll discuss this in-depth in chapter four.

You need to know that your WHY will change during your journey and that is okay. Your WHY may only get you through the first leg of your journey. You may need to reevaluate your WHY often and come up with a new WHY for the next leg. I know on one of my journeys my original WHY lasted me the entire time and on another journey, I was on, I had to come up with over five WHYs throughout the trip to keep me on track. Each WHY served its purpose. It's not that a WHY is bad — it just may need to be adjusted to get us through harder times.

I have learned that you need to find a WHY that makes you cry. Cry? Yes, cry. You need to dig deep and keep asking yourself why until you get to the root of your soul. Can you start with a shallow why? You bet. Here are some examples.

Let's say you want to lose weight and you're looking for a "why" to stay on track and keep eating healthy when you'd rather have that donut at the office that your vendor brings in every Friday.

What is my why?

I want to look hot in a swimsuit.

Why?

Because I'm tired of covering myself up at the pool because I'm ashamed of my body.

Why?

Because I've let myself go.

Why?

Because I feel horrible about myself.

Why?

Because I've been eating to numb the pain I feel.

Why?

Because I don't want to face the fact my marriage is falling apart.

Why?

Because…

You need to go as deep as you can until you truly feel that you have reached your *true* why. That ONE why that will hold you accountable. That one why that will keep you going on hard days.

And here's something you need to understand… sometimes your why changes! It does. It's okay to go through this exercise as many times as you need to find a new why. Take the time and go through the process when you feel the need to do so.

Let's run through this same process if your goal is to get out of debt. This is an actual exercise one of my clients shared with me.

What is my why?

I want to get out of debt.

Why?

Because I'm tired of the collection calls.

Why?

Because they make me feel horrible.

Why?

Because I'm mortified.

Why?

Because I'm afraid they'll find me at work or with my family or with friends.

Why?

Because I don't want anyone else to know how bad it is.

Why?

Because I feel like a failure.

Why?

Because my spending is out of control, and I can't seem to control it.

Why?

Because when I shop, I feel this "high," and it makes me feel powerful.

Why?

Because I feel powerless in the other areas of my life.

Why?

Because I let everyone walk all over me.

Why?

Because I'm a people pleaser.

Why?

Because I hate confrontation.

Why?

Because confrontation always turned to violence in my home growing up.

Why?

Because my parents didn't have the skillset to communicate clearly enough to each other.

Why?

Because their relationship was falling apart, and they just wanted to hurt each other.

Why?

Because…

Now, you can see that this example went way down deep. It went down to a point that had nothing to do with him but going through this exercise allowed him to find the train of thought that did mean something to him. Once he went through this process, he did it again with a little different direction. He kept the direction of the questions toward his own marriage and family.

What is my why?

I want to get out of debt.

Why?

Because I'm tired of the collection calls.

Why?

Because they make me feel horrible.

Why?

Because I'm mortified.

Why?

Because I'm afraid they'll find me at work or with my family or with friends.

Why?

Because I don't want anyone else to know how bad it is.

Why?

Because I feel like a failure.

Why?

Because my spending is out of control, and I can't seem to control it.

Why?

Because when I shop, I feel this "high," and it makes me feel powerful.

Why?

Because I feel powerless in the other areas of my life.

Why?

Because I let everyone walk all over me.

Why?

Because I'm a people pleaser.

Why?

Because I hate confrontation.

Why?

Because my wife and I need help learning how to communicate clearly.

Why?

Because we have both broken each other's trust financially and made poor decisions that have put us in financial ruin.

Why?

Because we both want the best things in life, but we can't afford them right now, but that doesn't stop us.

Why?

Because we want people to think we are better off than we are.

Why?

Because we're embarrassed that we don't have more by this time in our life.

Why?

Because we want people's respect.

Why?

Because we don't feel like we have anyone's respect.

Why?

Because we're both just us.

Why?

Because...

Do you see how redoing the work to take ownership will help you get to a why that can make a difference in your life and motivate you to stay on target to go after your dreams? Once he got to this point, he had an aha moment that he was doing the exact opposite of what he was trying to accomplish!

Discovering your WHY and unleashing its magical powers to chase after your dreams and goals is an empowering experience! It's like having a supercharged motivation booster on tap. When you figure out the reason that gets your heart racing and your spirit soaring, nothing can stop you. It's that inner fire that keeps you going when the going gets tough. Whether it's aiming for that dream job, starting your own business, conquering a new skill, or sacrificing to buy your dream car, knowing your WHY fuels you with passion and determination. It transforms your goals from daunting tasks into exciting adventures. So, dig deep, embrace your WHY with all your might, and let it lead you on the path to success!

DECLARATIONS

You may have heard about declarations before. You may have even used them before. That's great if you have! I hope you get back to using them daily. You may have also heard of affirmations. You may be wondering what's the difference between the two and does it really matter. Well, let's look at the difference and you can decide for yourself.

Let's review affirmations first. An affirmation is an act of saying or showing that something is true. Affirmation is when you are affirming something to be true by saying it. Perhaps you are affirming that you are loved, you are successful, you are enough. You need to feel that you are loved, that you are successful, or that you are enough. However, if you don't feel that you are these things, your energy won't support your words. Affirmations are useless when you can't feel them and believe in them. Whenever you are affirming something but deep down your mind is blocking the affirmation because you don't believe in it, it's better to not do the affirmation at all. You'll find yourself fighting yourself and even going backward in your goals when you affirm something that your mind and body can't get behind.

So, let's discuss declarations. A declaration is much stronger and much more powerful than an affirmation. A declaration is a powerful state of what you want to create. It's a commitment to a specific result. Declarations are powerful statements that can make you move from where you are now to where you want to be. They are made with the intention of up-leveling your life while creating and achieving the intended result.

Declarations are positive statements that may condition your mind so that you can develop a more positive perception of yourself. They help you achieve goals, and they can help you undo negative scripts that you repeatedly tell yourself. A declaration is a commitment to achieve the result you want. When you say your declaration, you have to do it with an intention to achieve it. You have to say it with passion. Declarations are not wishes, prayers, or hopes. Declarations are intentions or commitments.

What we say carries incredible power. We are bombarded daily with negative thoughts. Declarations help us put positive thoughts and intentions out into the world instead of negative ones.

Declarations don't need to be complicated. Let's go through a few variations so you can see what I mean.

One-Word Declarations

They can be as simple as a single word when we need a quick positive, reassuring thought. Simply pick a word that has significance to you. An example would be shouting out the word, "Abundance!" Pick a positive, action-oriented word to repeat as a mantra in moments when you need a quick pick-me-up. Consider having several words you can choose from.

About three years ago, I came up with three words that I wanted to become and declare. I chose "brave," "beautiful," and "compassionate." At the time, I wasn't accomplishing any of my dreams because I let fear overrule me. I felt horrible about myself, and my self-esteem was in the toilet. I also knew I needed to be kinder to my family. I was frustrated with my life and could see I would take my frustrations out on them.

I was challenged to set an alarm on my phone that would go off twice a day that said those three words on them. So at 9:15 a.m. and 9:15 p.m., an alarm would go off on my phone that said, "*Brave. Beautiful. Compassionate.*" Each time that alarm went off, I would stop and say to myself, *I am brave. I am beautiful. I am compassionate.* During the morning alarm, I would think of ways I could be brave, beautiful, and compassionate that day. During the evening alarm, I would take a moment to find ways I had been brave, beautiful, and compassionate. It didn't take long. One minute in the morning and one minute in the evening.

This was an incredible exercise. It didn't take long before I was no longer letting fear rule me. I started feeling better about myself and truly did feel beautiful. And most importantly to me, my relationship with my family improved by becoming more compassionate. It's been three years and I still have an alarm go off twice a day. Today my words are different, but the action is the same. Twice a day, I pause, say my declarations and take a moment to evaluate and be thankful for the opportunity to grow.

One-Sentence Declarations

While one-word declarations can bring you confidence and help with negative thoughts, getting more detailed can be a helpful step. Use sentence starters like "I am" or "I inspire." You can use these declarations throughout the day.

Declarations that take the form of statements are complete mind-changing thoughts. A one-sentence declaration can be as simple as, "I am a caring friend." Or, perhaps you want a more powerful one-sentence declaration. You could create something like, "I openly and outrageously express myself as a trusting, deserving, fearless leader." What matters is using them with feeling and that they mean something to you.

Multiple-Sentence Declarations

Having a one-word mantra or a simple sentence that you can rely on during the day is a powerful way to boost yourself to face daily challenges. You can also use a series of empowering statements. Five powerful statements around something that is meaningful to you and what are trying to accomplish is a great way to accomplish your goals. You can create your own set of five-sentence declarations or use someone else's list to get started. The idea is to boost your self-mastery. Using these declarations at least twice a day will boost your enthusiasm. Five-sentence declarations work best when you say them in front of the mirror, in the morning and evening. Say them loud and with high energy. Say them softly and with feeling. The more involved you get with these declarations, the more effective they will be.

Here are a few samples of possible five-sentence declarations you can use that I learned from my mentor, Kirk Duncan.

Let's say you want to master your influence. Five declarations you could say twice each day could be:

- *I add value to other people's lives.*
- *I am a great and powerful listener.*
- *I am confident and charismatic.*
- *I am a generous giver and an excellent receiver!*
- *I influence others to find their TRUTH!*

Perhaps you want to become better at presenting. You could use these five declarations:

- *I act with boldness and courage.*
- *I have rich knowledge and experience to share.*
- *My message is clear and direct.*
- *I inspire and engage the minds of the people.*

- *I am an excellent program designer.*

Here are ones I created as I wanted to increase my financial abundance:

- *I embrace abundance and it embraces me.*
- *I am abundant in every good way.*
- *I am an abundance magnet.*
- *I experience great victories.*
- *I manage my money wisely.*

Now, it's time to declare to yourself and the universe what you want to achieve. Each morning stand in front of your mirror proudly. Say your declarations out loud with confidence while looking yourself in the eye. Really try to *feel* what it is you are declaring.

Even if you currently don't believe that declarations work, you have nothing to lose if you just try to say them for a few weeks. Pay attention to how you feel when you are saying them and how you feel throughout the day as they come to mind during stressful times.

VISION BOARDS

The visual part of your brain is powerful! Do you get that? It. Is. Powerful!

I have been using a vision board since 2016 and it's incredible how much I have been able to manifest over the past seven years. I keep a binder of all the things I have been able to manifest from my vision board.

Are you thinking, "Whoa! This lady just lost her mind!"? I haven't, I promise. I know this sounds woo-woo. I get it. I thought it was woo-woo the first time I heard about it. But I am a true believer now! I'm not just a true believer, I'm a disciple. I use this tool with all of my clients. I have my vision board on the wall next to my desk so I can look at it multiple times a day.

Kirk Duncan at 3KeyElements taught me about vision boards and how to have success with them. He taught me how our minds work and how to put out to the universe what we want and that others will help us get what we want from our vision board. He says: "Every thought you have generates a feeling. Every feeling you have generates a body gesture or a movement. Every movement sends messages out to the world. Those messages going out to the world hit the people. The people get the message and then they respond to the message."

We all have a strong desire to create. Our vision board is our visualization of what it is that we want to create. When we are in creation mode, other people can sense that energy and they want to help us even if they don't know it consciously.

Here is the simplified version of creating a vision board right this minute. Get some green or blue painter's tape. Frame a 3-foot by 3-foot area with the tape. Take a post-it note and write what you want on it. Place it inside your vision board space. Find an image for what you want on that post-it note and put it next to it on your vision board. Then, each day, look at that post-it note for three minutes in the morning and three minutes in the evening. And that's it!

Whoa, Whoa, Whoa! I bet you think there is more to it than that. Well, there is! But I'm not going to go too deep into this because I HIGHLY encourage you to go to the link down in the resources and take the full training. It's free! It's great training and it will change your life. This is the program that taught me about vision board success. This free training is what taught me how to truly manifest all the things I now have and that I am continually updating for the next things I want to manifest.

DESIGNING A POWERFUL MORNING ROUTINE

How many times have you gone to bed with a STRONG desire to start something new the next day? Perhaps you want to start a new diet or start working out, or be a calmer parent. How many times have you gone to bed deciding that tomorrow will be the day, only to wake up and hit snooze, or start eating garbage for breakfast instead of the healthy meal you had planned out the night before? Everything you had thought about, planned for, and rededicated your time to just flew out the window.

Creating a morning routine is what will set you apart from others as you Design YOUR Dream Life Plan. You have goals you want to go after. You have dreams you want to come to fruition. Starting your morning each day with a powerful routine will allow you to increase your success rate.

Instead of waking up and allowing your feelings to dictate how good your day is going to be and what you are going to accomplish, create a routine that will set you up for success each and every day. You get to design the morning routine that works for you. Below is a list of options you could include in YOUR morning routine. Pick and choose what will work for you. Be willing to try things even if you don't see the value of them, yet.

- Prayer and/or meditation
- Declarations
- Vision board
- Journaling
- Gratitude list
- Envisioning
- Review goals and targets
- Reviewing YOUR rules

Some of these routines are clear and obvious, but let's go through some of the routines that might be new to you.

Envisioning. There is power in imagining your future self and visualizing what you desire becoming a reality. It's been said that what you envision, you can achieve. Envisioning your dreams will help you gain clarity about what you want to accomplish. This is not about figuring out how it will happen. This is about deciding what you want and gaining the clarity you need to set goals and achieve success. Envisioning is different from dreaming. Envisioning is about facing the reality of what you can achieve based on the choices you are making. Envisioning gives you something to focus on.

Envisioning the success you desire and focusing on how you will feel once you achieve your goal will alleviate some of the pain of discipline in the here and now. It also helps you keep your eye on the ball, or in our case, your eye on the road to your dreams.

Reviewing YOUR Rules. Craig Ballantyne is the creator of The Perfect Day Formula. In his program, he discusses the need to define your set of rules that you will live by each and every day. Craig's program teaches you how structure equals freedom, how to control your mornings, conquer the chaos of your day, and concentrate on what really matters. Creating rules that will become your life's map is very important and a great thing to review every morning to remind yourself of your priorities and to set your day up for success.

You may be wondering what the rules might look like. Here are the rules I've created for myself and have been operating under for many years. I have updated it occasionally as needed and keep a copy on my wall above my monitor to remind me every day what my guiding principles are.

1. I go to bed and get up at the same time every day (10:30 p.m. and 6:30 a.m.).

2. When I wake up, I am organized and in control of my actions. There is a purpose and goal in my head and heart each morning.

3. I work on myself first thing every morning.
    a. I take care of myself physically by following a healthy diet every day.
    b. I take care of myself spiritually by:
        i. Reading my scriptures daily
        ii. Praying each morning and evening with intention and gratitude
    c. I take care of myself emotionally by:
        i. Slaying my dragons every day

ii. Filling my own buckets for love & connection, variety, significance, certainty, growth & contribution

4. I work on my productivity plan today in preparation for tomorrow by planning tomorrow's tasks and schedule, updating my gratitude & achievement journals, and journaling at the end of each day.

5. I do not check emails before 10 a.m. so that I have time to work on what is important to me and what I already have outlined to do without having to react to others' issues. I stay off social media until lunch.

6. I do not binge-watch shows. I limit my watching to 2 episodes a week. I want to spend my time creating my dreams, not wasting my life.

7. I am guided by these phrases:
   a. **"Do it with Passion, or Not at All."** — I don't believe in doing anything halfway. I will give every project I work on my very best and will choose only projects that spur my passion and bring me closer to my goals.
   b. **"I Can Do Hard Things."** — I know I can do hard things when I am following God's plan for me. So, I will make every decision with God. I know that by following the plan He wants me to follow, I cannot lose.
   c. **"Persistence Trumps Talent."** — I know that being willing to work hard, learn new things, and keep moving forward will pay off in the end.
   d. **"This Too Shall Pass."** — There will still be trials, so I will need to persevere. But I know that I will be led to ways to overcome each trial that arises because I'm following God's plan.

e. **"If I'm not winning, I'm learning."** — I recognize that I will have many opportunities to learn, and I look forward to each and every one.

8. I take personal responsibility for my life — everything that happens to me — both good and bad. I blame no one but myself. These are the choices I've made. This is the life I'm living. I accept the consequences of my actions.

9. I will be the person I want my family and clients to be — decisive, hardworking, kind to others, willing to learn and grow, seeing the good in others and God's hand in everything. I act politely and courteously to all. I am patient with my family and others and choose my battles with care.

10. I make time to laugh and play with my family every day.

11. I am a champion to others. If appropriate, I find ways to help others find their passions and live their dreams.

Some of these rules may resonate for you, and some won't. That's okay! This is why they are MY rules, not yours. You get to create your own rules that will resonate, motivate, and propel you to continue going after YOUR dreams.

HIRING COACHES

"Good Coaches share lessons from their experience. Great coaches help you crystalize lessons from your experience. Good Coaches give us useful answers. Great coaches help you ask better questions. Good coaches walk you through their path. Great coaches help you identify your path."

— Adam Grant

Working with a coach can be extremely beneficial for several reasons:

1. Clarity and Goal-Setting: A coach can help you clarify your goals and identify what you truly want to achieve in your personal or professional life. They can also help you set goals that will help you get there.
2. Accountability: A coach can help you stay accountable to your goals and commitments. By regularly checking in with you and helping you stay on track, a coach can help you achieve more than you might have on your own.
3. Support and Encouragement: A coach can provide you with emotional support and encouragement, especially during difficult times. They can help you stay motivated and focused on your goals, even when you face setbacks or obstacles.
4. Objectivity and Feedback: A coach can provide you with objective feedback on your performance, behavior, and mindset. They can help you identify blind spots and areas for improvement that you may not be aware of on your own.
5. Skill Development: A coach can help you develop and improve new skills. They can provide you with guidance, resources, and feedback to help you become more effective in your personal or professional life.

Working with a coach can help you gain clarity, stay accountable, receive emotional support, and develop new skills. By working with a coach, you can achieve your goals more effectively and efficiently than you would on your own.

Hiring a coach must be the number one success tool in my toolkit. Coaches have defined me, changed my trajectory, and improved my life in ways I can't imagine. They have impacted my life forever.

Coaches aid their clients in improving their relationships, careers, and day-to-day lives. Life coaches can help you clarify your goals, identify the obstacles holding you back, and then help you develop strategies for overcoming each obstacle.

One of the main benefits of working with a coach is the ability to gain a fresh, informed perspective on problems you face. In addition to offering new insight into challenges, a coach can help you to zero in on negative patterns that could be standing in the way of your success. Many people view working with a coach as bridging the gap between your current circumstances and the life you'd like to lead.

I've worked with some great coaches as well as some mediocre coaches. I learned something from each of them, but the great ones truly skyrocketed me to the next level from where I was, and I am eternally grateful for them.

I started coaching couples on getting out of debt by accident. A friend knew my accounting background and that my husband and I were in a good place financially. She asked if I could help her and her husband get their finances in order. I met with them and created a game plan, and sent them on their way. I checked in on them each month and saw that they weren't doing the work like we had outlined. We worked on why they were struggling and revamped the game plan. It worked better for them. They worked better on the plan and saw great success. They were very happy and recommended a family member reach out, and they did. And the rest, as they say, is history. I've been helping couples by word of mouth for the past 19 years. It has been very rewarding. I have literally saved marriages by helping them get their finances in order! I love what I do and want to continue to grow and serve more people.

The great coaches I have worked with created a strong desire for me to hone my skills and learn to become a better coach myself. My journey has taken me to become a certified personal empowerment coach, as well as a master practitioner of NLP (Neuro-Linguistic Programming) and Time Line Therapy®, a master hypnosis practitioner, and NLP coach. I now have more tools in my tool belt to help more people. I love being able to help someone that is stuck and provide them with the tools they need to see massive results.

I am grateful for the coaches I have worked with and for the time they took to hone their skills. I have taken what I have learned from each and incorporated them into my personal life, my family's lives, and my businesses. I have been able to make a difference in others' lives because they were able to make a difference in mine.

I have learned the importance of finding people who have accomplished what I want and learning from their experiences. I have also learned the importance and power of coaching and will never not have a coach to help me on my journey. Coaches are the ultimate pit crew on my journey!

I'd like to share with you some of the GREAT coaches I have personally worked with, what I learned from them, what they helped me accomplish to get to where I am today, and how to start learning from them immediately.

Richie Norton

Known For:

Bestselling author of the books *The Power of Starting Something Stupid,* and *Anti-Time Management.*

Partial Bio:

He is the award-winning, bestselling author of the books *The Power of Starting Something Stupid* (in 10+ languages) and *Résumés Are Dead & What to Do About It.* In 2019, Richie was named one of the world's top 100 business coaches by Dr. Marshall Goldsmith. He is an international speaker (including TEDx & Google Startup Grind) and serial entrepreneur.

What I learned from Him:

Richie was my first coach, and you never forget your first. He set the bar high for every other coach I will ever hire. He taught me how to determine what my true passion in life was and how to have the courage to go after my dreams. He taught my business partner and me some great business acumen that has helped with every other business I have started. He was a great cheerleader when we really needed it. He made personal introductions to some very strong partnerships to help our business grow and scale.

Introduction:

Read the book, *The Power of Starting Something Stupid,* and/or, *Anti-Time Management*

Sign up for this 76-Day Challenge to make your STUPID idea Your SMART Reality at http://richienorton.com/76daychallenge/

Kirk Duncan

Known for:

Master Your Influence Program

Partial Bio:

President and founder of 3 Key Elements and member of the National Speakers Association, Kirk has developed his company from a card table in the garage into a multi-million-dollar, award-winning company. 3 Key Elements has been recognized for four consecutive years by Inc. 5000 as one of the fastest-growing companies in America. Kirk Duncan has given over 5,800 presentations, appeared on television 75 times, and regularly trains audiences of 200-900 students.

What I learned:

It's not an exaggeration when I say that Kirk saved my life and my marriage and put me on a trajectory I could never have imagined. His mindset training pulled me out of a deep, dark place I didn't even recognize I had fallen into until he showed me the light. I was profoundly and irrevocably changed in a room with over 1,000 people. I attended every class he put on in 2017 and 2018. These three-day classes taught me so much! I attended:

Present Yourself to learn public speaking

The Art of Mentoring as an introduction to coaching

Royalty and Romance to improve my marriage

Queen of the Kingdom with his wife, Kim Duncan, to find my feminine side

I invested in *The Elite* program, a 12-week program to define my personal coaching program. To this day, the tools I learned from Kirk sparked unimaginable levels of personal and professional growth, and I couldn't be more grateful. Kirk taught me how to go after what I want and the shortcuts to getting what I want. Much of what I'm teaching you today I learned from Kirk.

Introduction:

Check out his Master Your Influence group coaching at https://3keyelements.com/master-your-influence-join-today/

Listen to any of his audiobook trainings at https://3keyelements.com/audiobook-library/

Natasha Hazlett

Known for:

Bestselling Author of *Unstoppable Influence: Be You. Be Fearless. Transform Lives.*

Partial Bio:

Natasha empowers solopreneurs and aspiring solopreneurs with the clarity, confidence, training, and resources they need to BOOST their income and influence in the marketplace by monetizing their message online.

In addition to being an inspirational speaker, author, coach, and life changer, she's an award-winning internet marketer, attorney and co-founder of Fast Forward Marketing, LLC. The Idaho Business Review honored her with the 2013 Idaho Women of the Year Award.

What I learned:

Like Kirk, Natasha has irrevocably changed my life. From her 21-day Unstoppable Influencer Challenge, I discovered the lies I was telling myself that kept me stuck and no longer moving forward on my journey. It was like I had that darn tire boot on me and struggled in my business. I wanted to take it to the next level and could never gain any traction. I was spinning out and stuck.

Natasha taught me the power of divine timing. Everything happens for a reason at the time that I need it to happen for *me*. I'm working at a higher level than I was when I was with Kirk, and she has taken my mindset to the level it needs to be for where I am now. I am in the middle of my second year of being in her Inner Circle coaching program, which has skyrocketed my mindset and my skill set. She has given me power tools for my tool collection. I credit her coaching for me getting *two* book deals this year! She made introductions to influential people I would never normally have access to and allowed me a chance to grow personally as well as in my business.

Introduction:

Check her out at https://natashahazlett.com

Join her next 5-day Unstoppable Influence Challenge at https://unstoppableInfluence.idevaffiliate.com/2194.html

Michael Yeung

Known For:

Creator of Productivity and Performance Coaching

Partial Bio:

Michael Yeung is a high-performance coach and business consultant who specializes in helping entrepreneurs to achieve more with less.

With the help of his mentors as well as lessons learned from countless trial and error, he managed to unlock the secrets to maximizing one's return-on-time investment in the world of business. Leading him to evolve from a struggling entrepreneur trapped in constant overwhelm and anxiety to building a thriving business within a year.

What I learned:

The biggest lesson Michael has taught me is to focus on tasks that move the needle instead of tasks that make me feel important but are wasting my time, wearing me out, and not moving my business forward. You may recognize that many of us take great pride in being busy even though we are not accomplishing anything. Michael helps me see the forest through the trees. I have spent years chasing shiny things. I've dabbled. I've pivoted, thinking I'm making smart decisions. I've gotten in my own way too many times to count. Michael has been able to help me see why those decisions won't ultimately help me to reach my destination. He is a master at seeing how I'm getting in my own way again and again and getting me back on the right path to success.

Introduction:

Check out his website at https://www.eliteproductivity.io/

Join his free Facebook group at www.facebook.com/groups/teamppe

I hope you can see why working with a coach might be a great option for you as you go after your dreams and create your Dream Life Plan. There are coaches for almost any situation and goal you have. Do your research! Find one that you resonate with, and then do the work!

RESOURCES

Vision Board Training

BOOK RECOMMENDATIONS

Unstoppable Influence: Be You. Be Fearless. Transform Lives.
by Natasha Hazlett

The Perfect Day Formula, by Craig Ballantyne

ACTION MAP

1. Work through all the exercises for this chapter in the *Go For It!* Companion Workbook
2. Complete the vision board training at https://3keyelements.com/vision-board-training/
3. Read *Unstoppable Influence: Be You. Be Fearless. Transform Lives.*
4. Read *The Perfect Day Formula*

CHAPTER FIVE

The Law of the Mirror

"Do unto others as you would have them do unto you."
– The Golden Rule, Matthew 7:12

When you are on a journey in your car, you have tools that help you understand what is happening around you. Your rearview and side view mirrors help you see what is coming up around you and where you have been. There are many quotes about why the rearview mirror is smaller than the windshield. Though there are many versions; my favorite is by Max Lucado, who says, "*There is a reason the windshield is bigger than the rearview mirror. Your future matters more than your past.*"

"Your future matters more than your past." Wow! Think about that for a moment. Think of all the rags-to-riches stories of people who came from nothing or were told they would never succeed, who are now rich and famous. Just off the top of my head, I can think of several. Oprah was born super poor, was abused by family members, and ran away from home. She was smart and was awarded a scholarship to Tennessee State University. She became a TV correspondent at 19 and then went on to own and produce her own talk show, "The Oprah Winfrey Show." She is now worth over $2.6 billion. Michael Jordan didn't make his high school sophomore varsity team at 15. Many think he was cut, but it's come out that he never made the team in the first place.

Not making the team motivated him to practice harder and to work out more to bulk up. Now Michael Jordan is one of the best-known NBA players of all time, even long after he retired.

I bring these examples up because there are things you have been told by people, including yourself, that keep you from going after your dreams. There are parts of your past that have made you think that you aren't worthy. There are parts of your past that you don't want anyone to know about, so you don't want to put yourself out there. I want to ensure you don't let your past stop you from pursuing your dreams. I want you to realize how incredible you are and the very thing that is keeping you back is the very thing people need to see you overcome and will help you be the successful person I know you can be.

Mirrors are simply a reflection of what is in front of them. They reflect accurately, maintaining the same relative size and position of the objects reflected. Mirrors are used for more than just ensuring our hair and makeup look good. You may have heard the phrase, "Hold a mirror up to." The phrase means to take a look at oneself objectively to examine or reflect on things (issues) stemming from the reality of reflection or to expose and bring to light some (usually unpleasant) aspects of oneself. There are many times in life we need to hold the mirror up to ourselves and reflect on what is working and not working in our lives.

In 2016, I was working with a client who was frustrated with life. Both his marriage and business were struggling. He was on the verge of losing both. He was stressed about both and was making poor decisions about everything. As we talked one day, I asked him to tell me how he lived his life. He didn't quite understand what I was asking and asked for clarification. I asked him specifically, "How are you living your life? Do you have an attitude of gratitude? Do you look for ways to help others, or are you always looking for ways to take advantage of people? Do you seek to help or be helped?" He looked at me for a moment as he processed my questions. I wasn't shocked by his answers, but he sure was!

He told me that he was always looking for an edge to get ahead. He didn't care who was affected by it as long as it wasn't him. When I asked him to tell me more about what was going on with his business, he told me that his clients were "nickeling and diming him to death." It didn't matter what it was about, they wanted a better deal. I asked him if he was "nickeling and diming other people to death?" At first, he answered with a resounding NO! But as he sat there, he started realizing he was doing that at every opportunity. He told me he had recently gone shopping for a new washer and dryer. He said he haggled and haggled over the price of it and looked for every single incentive he could find to drive the price down. He told me he loved walking out of there knowing he hadn't been "taken advantage of," and he didn't care that the salesman lost some commission because of the way he did business.

We sat there for a moment in silence. I watched as his mind mulled over the event. He sat there very proud of himself for what he had accomplished to get the very best deal on that washer and dryer set. Then as we sat there, I saw his mind go through the event and start piecing things together. Suddenly, he looked at me with an incredulous look of insight and then horror. It was the perfect time to teach him the Law of the Mirror.

As I sat there with my client, I asked him to tell me again about how his clients were behaving. He looked down at his hands and clenched his fists a few times. He looked back at me and sheepishly said, "Exactly as I'm behaving with others." Yes!

John C. Maxwell's Law of the Mirror comes from his book, *The 15 Invaluable Laws of Growth: Live Them and Reach Your Potential.* His Law of the Mirror states "You must see value in yourself to add value in yourself." The Law of the Mirror is about building self-esteem. It's about strengthening your belief in yourself. It's also about adding value to others.

I told my client that he needed to become his ideal client. When he asked me what that meant, I told him he needed to be the person he wanted others to be toward him.

I introduced him to the Law of the Mirror in Business:

- If you want decisive action-taking clients, you need to be decisive and act.
- If you want to get paid on time and not have to chase money to get paid, you need to pay your bills on time.
- If you want case studies, testimonials, and positive client experiences, you must be the first person to give others case studies, testimonials, and positive client experiences.
- If you want your clients to follow instructions, you must follow instructions and quit trying to kick against the pricks all the time.
- If you want clients to see value in your work, you must start seeing the value in the work others provide.
- If you don't want your clients to nickel and dime you to death, quit nickeling and diming everyone you try to work with.

After going through these examples, I asked him if he could see how powerful the Law of the Mirror could be. I asked him if he could see how looking at how he was doing business could change the trajectory of it.

This may sound like rhetoric to you, but I promise you, if you start really changing your attitude about how you do business, your clients will change their minds about how they do business with you. People do business with people that are like them. You have complete control over the type of clients you attract.

I also wanted to use the Law of the Mirror to help my client with his marriage. I asked him again how he was living his life, but this time I wanted him to focus on his relationship with his wife and kids. He told me that his wife was always upset, his kids spoke rudely to him, and he hated going home at night. I asked him how using the Law of the Mirror principles might help his personal life. I asked him to develop some ideas using the Law of the Mirror that might help him improve his relationships with the most important people in his life.

This is the list he came up with that day for the Law of the Mirror in his life:

- If I want my family to be kind to me, I must be kind to them.
- If I want my kids to speak to me respectfully, I must show them respect.
- If I want my wife to be happy, I must find ways to show my love for her.
- If I want a happy marriage, I must show up lovingly every day.
- If I want my time at home to be pleasant, I must be pleasant to be around.

How are you living your life with the most important people to you? Are you seeing negative or positive patterns in your relationship? If they are negative, can you see how using the Law of the Mirror could help you improve those relationships? Do you need to list laws to live by for your life?

I am happy to report that my client saw immediate improvements in his business and personal life as he started living with the Law of the Mirror in mind.

As I previously mentioned, the Law of the Mirror is about building self-esteem and strengthening your belief in yourself. There is another incident that happened about nine years ago that has stuck with me. I think this story will help illustrate the importance of this principle.

Years ago, I purchased a used Total Gym online. I paid $100 for it. I brought it home, used it for about a month, then dusted it for several years. Does anyone else do that, or just me? LOL.

I finally admitted to myself that I was never going to use it again and went online to sell it. When I looked, there were two other Total Gyms for sale. One asked $25 for theirs, and the other asked $30. Both ads had been on there for several weeks. Knowing I had paid $100 for mine and it was still in great shape, I wasn't willing to go that low. I knew it was a risk, but I listed my Total Gym for $100 "firm." And you know what? I sold it the same day!

Those two other Total Gyms for a lot less money were still for sale after weeks, but mine sold immediately at a much higher price. Why? I saw value in my Total Gym, so others saw its value. The other people didn't see value in theirs, so no one else did either.

Can you see why it is important to find value in yourself? If you want people to find value in you, you must find value in what you have to offer others. Zig Ziglar says, *"It's impossible to consistently behave in a manner inconsistent with how we see ourselves. We can do very few things in a positive way if we feel negative about ourselves."*

How can you build your self-esteem and strengthen your belief in yourself? How can you create positive feelings about yourself to feel confident enough to go after your dreams?

John Maxwell lists 10 steps to Build Your Self-Image.

1. Guard your self-talk.
2. Stop comparing yourself to others.
3. Move beyond your limiting beliefs.
4. Add value to others.
5. Do the right thing, even if it's the hard thing.
6. Practice a small discipline daily in a specific area of your life.
7. Celebrate small victories.
8. Embrace a positive vision for your life based on what you value.
9. Practice the one-word strategy.
10. Take responsibility for your life.

You matter. Your story matters. You have something inside you that others need. You feel that there is something that you should be doing that will make a difference to many people as well as yourself. You must build your self-esteem and self-image to go after your dreams. I hope you will take the time to do so.

There is a quote by Marianne Williamson that I love and have had on my wall by my desk for years that I hope will serve you.

Our deepest fear is not that we are inadequate.

Our deepest fear is that we are powerful beyond measure.

It is our light, not our darkness that most frightens us.

We ask ourselves, "Who am I to be brilliant, gorgeous, talented, fabulous?"

Actually, who are you not to be?

You are a child of God.

Your playing small does not serve the world.

There is nothing enlightened about shrinking so that other people won't feel insecure around you.

We are all meant to shine, as children do.

We were born to make manifest the glory of God that is within us.

It's not just in some of us; it's in everyone.

And as we let our own light shine, we unconsciously give other people permission to do the same.

As we are liberated from our own fear, our presence automatically liberates others.

This world needs more light right now. It doesn't need more darkness. It doesn't need more fear.

It needs light! It needs people coming out, being their authentic selves, and making a difference because people are searching for it. They are begging for it. They're desperate for it. They're searching for YOU!

So don't be afraid anymore!

BOOK RECOMMENDATIONS

The 15 Invaluable Laws of Growth: Live Them and Reach Your Potential, by John C. Maxwell

ACTION MAP

1. Work through all the exercises for this chapter in the *Go For It!* Companion Workbook
2. Reflect on how things are going in your life and decide if some changes are in order.
3. Read *The 15 Invaluable Laws of Growth: Live Them and Reach Your Potential*

CHAPTER SIX

How Your Attitude & Feelings Determine Your Financial Success

"A bad attitude is like a flat tire. You won't get anywhere until you change it." **— Zig Ziglar**

I'm frantically knocking on wood right now as I realize I don't have a personal story about a flat tire. Apparently, I have been blessed and haven't had to deal with that. As I've looked for other people's stories about flat tires, nothing really resonated. But I did find a site that had a few jokes about flat tires. I thought I'd share a couple here. One thing to know about me… I LOVE a good dad joke or pun. You know, the kind that makes you roll your eyes and go, "Oh, brother!" My kids and I share puns and dad jokes on our group chat and laugh like crazy. So here you go… Sorry, not sorry!

Tell me a flat tire joke... No pressure

"What did the vegetarian say when they were stranded with a flat tire?"
Should have brought asparagus.

"What happens when a frog gets a flat tire?"
He gets toad.

"Two blondes are looking at a flat tire. One asks the other, *How bad is it?*

The other says, *Not bad, it's only flat on the bottom.*"

"How many Kansas City Chiefs does it take to change a flat tire?"
Just one. Unless it's a blowout, then the whole team shows up.

Me: "I went 365 days without having a single incident of a flat tire. It was a Goodyear."
The tire man: "Remember to rotate your tires."
Me: "Don't they rotate themselves when we drive?"

"When the mystery machine gets a flat tire, who has to change it?"
Scooby Doo.

"I have a joke about a flat tire... But I'll spare you from it."

"The pessimist had a flat tire... so he opened the trunk and pulled out despair."

Okay, okay... enough. I hope you still like me after this.

Your attitude and feelings play a significant role in determining your financial success. How you think and feel about money can influence your financial decisions and actions, ultimately impacting your financial outcome.

Your attitude toward money affects how you handle it. If you have a negative attitude towards money, you may be more likely to spend it impulsively, accumulate debt, or avoid managing it altogether. However, if you have a positive attitude toward money, you may be more likely to save, invest, and make smart financial decisions.

Furthermore, your feelings about money can affect your confidence and motivation to succeed financially. If you feel anxious or stressed about money, you may avoid making financial decisions, which can lead to missed opportunities for growth and success. On the other hand, if you feel empowered and confident about your financial situation, you are more likely to take risks and pursue financial goals.

Your mindset also plays a critical role in determining your financial success. A fixed mindset can limit your ability to grow and improve your financial situation, while a growth mindset can empower you to learn, adapt, and succeed.

For example, a person with a fixed mindset may believe they are not good with money and will always struggle financially, leading to a self-fulfilling prophecy. In contrast, a person with a growth mindset may recognize that they have room for improvement and actively seek out opportunities to learn and grow their financial knowledge and skills.

Ultimately, your attitude and feelings toward money can impact your financial success. By cultivating a positive attitude and growth mindset toward money, you can increase your confidence, motivation, and ability to make smart financial decisions that lead to long-term success.

This chapter in the workbook will be significant for you as you explore your current feelings about money and how to let go of things you were taught that aren't working for you to create a healthier relationship with money that supports you in going after your dreams.

While this chapter is specifically about your attitude toward money, this can be applied the same way in going after your dreams. Are you open to growth and learning new things? The workbook will take you through exercises about going after your dreams as well as your finances.

BOOK RECOMMENDATIONS

Attitude 101 by John C. Maxwell

ACTION MAP

1. Work through all the exercises for this chapter in the *Go For It!* Companion Workbook
2. Read *Attitude 101*

Jokes and puns from this chapter came from https://upjoke.com/flat-tire-jokes and https://kidadl.com/funnies/puns/hilarious-tire-puns-that-wont-fall-flat and https://punstoppable.com/flat-tire-puns

CHAPTER SEVEN

Financial Literacy Basics

***"Patience is something you admire in the driver behind you and scorn in the one ahead."* — Mac McCleary**

"Wait… What?" – My teenage son all day, every day.

I love my son. He cracks me up. He comes up with the most random, hilarious stuff daily. Right now, he's in the "Wait… What?" phase, which means he's kind of paying attention, but not really, so things catch him off guard, and it's funny to watch him catch up in a conversation.

You may be saying, "Wait… what?" right now as I just transitioned to financial literacy in a book about going after your dreams. But just like my son, you can probably figure out quickly why financial literacy is vital to going after your dreams. In truth, it's actually the foundation to support and sustain you in going after your dreams.

When you build a house, or any structure for that matter, if the foundation isn't set correctly, it will eventually start having issues. A poor foundation causes secondary problems. If your foundation isn't solid, your house could settle, and you'll have issues like cracked walls, uneven floors, doors that won't close, and many others.

Not having a strong financial foundation will prevent you from truly going after your dreams. Most businesses fail because of a lack of capital. Your inability to create a strong financial foundation will prevent you from reaching your goals and dreams. I don't want to see that happen to you.

I want to help you create a solid foundation that will support each and every dream you decide to go after. Understanding the basics of finance will put you ahead of most people. Banks and investment firms like to make money sound more complicated than it is to ensure you feel you need them. They have mastered the idea of using other people's money to make money. When you are uneducated and default to just putting your money in the bank, they use it to make money for themselves and give you pennies on the dollar. I want you to be so comfortable with money that you know how to earn it, grow it, invest it, and how to create a solid foundation for yourself, not for others.

FINANCIAL LITERACY

A standard car, or a manual transmission car, requires the driver to change gears using a clutch pedal and gearshift manually. The clutch pedal is pressed down to disengage the engine from the transmission, and the driver shifts gears using the gearshift lever. This requires the driver to use both feet and hands to control the vehicle.

On the other hand, an automatic car has an automatic transmission that shifts gears automatically as the vehicle accelerates or decelerates. This means that the driver does not need to use a clutch pedal or gearshift lever. Instead, the car's computer system manages the gear changes, allowing the driver to use only their feet to control the vehicle.

The main difference between these two types of cars is the level of control the driver has over the gear changes. In a standard car, the driver has full control over the gear changes and can choose when to shift gears. In an automatic car, the car's computer system takes care of the gear changes, making driving easier and less physically demanding. However, some drivers prefer the control and engagement that comes with driving a standard car, while others find automatic cars more convenient and less stressful to drive.

Growing up, my mom drove a standard transmission 1979 Diesel Volkswagen Rabbit. It had a whopping 71 horsepower engine. Aww yeah!! When it was time to learn how to drive, my mom handed the keys to my BFF and said, "Here, you can teach her." My friend drove me to the local junior college with a massive empty parking lot. We traded places, and my friend taught me how to drive a stick shift that day. We went up and down that parking lot. I ground the gears, did many brutal hard stops and a lot of rough starts, and we laughed the entire time because no one was getting frustrated or worried about their car. It was a perfect way to learn to drive!

After I got the hang of things more, she took me onto the road to drive home. It was a LONG drive home, but we survived. A few weeks later, I was taking my sister somewhere and had done well driving around town. Then for some unknown reason, I stalled the car at a light. The light cycled, and I had cars honking at me. My hands began to sweat. I sat at that light, repeatedly stalling for SIX light cycles! I had been honked at, sped by, flipped off, and yelled at. I was sweating in more places than my hands when I finally got through that intersection. I can still remember the stress of that experience over 35 years later. Interestingly enough, that was the last time I ever stalled the car. I got so good driving that standard transmission that I could stop and hold it on a hill, balancing the clutch and gas pedal, never touching the brake. I loved driving and being in control! Driving became my stress release. Even though that little Rabbit only had 71 horsepower, I knew how to drive it and drive it well.

Now that I'm older, I enjoy driving my automatic transmission. I'm glad I learned on a standard and have that skill. It has kept me from becoming limited in what I could do as an adult. I think everyone should know how to drive a standard transmission. Fun fact: I even thought about starting a driving school for licensed people who just wanted to learn to drive a standard transmission.

You may be asking what in the world analyzing a standard transmission versus an automatic transmission has to do with finances. And I'm glad you're asking that. Because I think it is a perfect analogy for how you need to learn to take control of your money. Many people are scared of money. They feel ignorant and don't think they are smart enough to really learn about it. Banks and investment managers want you to feel that way. They want you ignorant, so you'll just give them your money.

I, on the other hand, want you to be educated about money. I want you to be confident and in control. I want you to drive your money just like a manual transmission. You decide how you'll handle it. You decide how you'll spend it. You decide how you'll invest it. Knowledge is power and brings confidence. That is what I want for you. I want you to learn how to master your finances so no one can exploit you.

Later in life, you can change your money tactics, if you want, to automatic, but not until you are ready and you know what it really means to do so.

ABCs OF FINANCIAL LITERACY

Understanding the ABCs of financial literacy will help you create a solid foundation that will help you obtain your dreams. You may think you already know these, but I recommend you go through them anyway. It's quick, it's informative, and it's possible you may get a new perspective to create the solid foundation you need.

A is for... ***Asset.***

An asset is anything that has value and can be owned. In finance and accounting, an asset is defined as a resource controlled by an individual, corporation, or government that is expected to provide future economic benefit. Assets can take many forms, including physical assets such as real estate and equipment, financial assets such as stocks, bonds, and cash, and intangible assets such as intellectual property and goodwill. The main characteristic of an asset is that it has value and can be used to generate income or support the production of goods and services.

B is for… ***Budget.***

A family budget is a financial plan that outlines the income and expenses of a household so it can manage its money effectively. It helps families prioritize their spending, track their expenses, and ensure they are spending within their means. A family budget typically includes categories such as housing, food, transportation, healthcare, entertainment, and savings. The goal of a family budget is to ensure that the family is living within its means and saving for the future while still having enough money for the things that are important to them.

Ahhh, the dreaded "B" word. Most people HATE that word. It immediately makes them think of being broke. However, a budget is the backbone of a successful personal financial plan. And not just personal. Businesses use budgets all the time to reach their goals and to create financial success. A budget is simply a blueprint or map to your financial success. Instead of reacting to emergencies, a budget allows you to prepare in advance for unexpected issues and makes your money work for you instead of you working for it. At the time of this writing, CreditDonkey.com reports that only 32% of U.S. households prepare a monthly budget, and out of those who budget, 70% take the time to check their spending against it once a week.

Creating a budget can be scary. People know they may not be in a great financial position, and the thought of putting it down on paper to see it in black and white can become almost debilitating. Budgets also make people feel constricted and prevent them from enjoying life.

Budgeting is all about mindset and perception. There are many reasons people don't want to budget. Some include: Budgeting can encourage a restrictive mindset around money. You will sabotage your best plans and set yourself up for failure. On the flip side, if you can see a budget as simply a powerful tool to take control of your money and help you reach your dreams faster, you'll enjoy it and keep using it. I want to show you how that dreaded "B" word is actually the best tool to use to reach your dreams, whatever they may be.

C is for... ***Cash, Credit, Capital***

Cash refers to physical currency, coins, and banknotes, that is commonly used as a medium of exchange for goods and services. It is a tangible asset that can be easily traded for goods and services without the need for a bank or other financial institution. Cash is widely accepted as a form of payment and is often used for day-to-day transactions.

Credit is the ability to borrow money or goods and services with the understanding that they will be repaid in the future, usually with interest. It is a financial instrument that allows individuals, businesses, and organizations to obtain loans and make purchases without having to pay upfront. The credit may come from banks, credit unions, credit card companies, or other financial institutions. The creditworthiness of an individual or business is determined by factors such as income, credit history, and the ability to repay the loan.

Capital refers to the resources, such as money, equipment, property, and investments, that are used to produce goods and services and generate income. Capital can also refer to the financial assets, such as stocks and bonds, invested to earn a return. Capital is a key component in the creation of wealth and is essential for economic growth and development.

D is for... ***Debt, Discipline, Diversification***

Debt is an amount of money owed by an individual or organization to another entity, typically as a result of borrowing funds. It is the sum of money that must be repaid with interest in accordance with the terms of a loan agreement. Debts can be incurred in a variety of ways, such as through loans, mortgages, credit card balances, or other forms of borrowing. The goal of debt is usually to finance the purchase of goods or services, invest in a project or business, or to achieve a specific financial goal.

Discipline refers to the actions and attitudes that promote control, order, and obedience in a person or a group. It involves setting and maintaining rules, expectations, and standards of behavior. It may involve punishment or reward, but it is primarily aimed at helping individuals or groups to develop self-control and improve their performance.

Diversification is a strategy of spreading investments across multiple different asset classes, industries, or geographic regions in order to reduce the risk of loss and increase the chances of positive returns. By diversifying, investors aim to balance their portfolios and minimize the impact of market fluctuations or sector-specific events that could cause harm to their investments. Diversification can be achieved by investing in stocks, bonds, real estate, commodities, or other asset classes.

E is for… ***Economics, Education, Expenses***

Economics is a social science that deals with the production, consumption, and distribution of goods and services. It studies the behavior and decision-making of individuals, businesses, and governments and their impact on markets and the economy as a whole. Economics also examines how societies allocate limited resources among unlimited wants and needs. It covers a wide range of topics, including microeconomics (the behavior of individual consumers and firms), macroeconomics (the behavior of the economy as a whole), international economics (the relationship between countries and trade), and public economics (the role of government in the economy).

Education is the process of acquiring knowledge, skills, values, beliefs, and habits through various forms of learning and teaching. It involves learning in a structured and systematic manner, usually through formal institutions such as schools, colleges, and universities. Education helps individuals develop their intellectual and personal capacities and prepares them for their societal role. The ultimate goal of education is to equip individuals with the skills, knowledge, and attitudes they need to live fulfilling and productive lives.

Personal **Expenses** are the money spent on individual needs, wants, and leisure activities. They are expenses incurred by individuals for their own personal use and do not include business or work-related expenses. Examples of personal expenses include:

- Housing expenses (rent or mortgage, utilities, insurance, property taxes)
- Food and grocery expenses
- Clothing and personal grooming expenses
- Transportation costs (fuel, parking, public transportation)
- Health and fitness expenses (doctor visits, gym memberships)
- Entertainment expenses (movies, concerts, hobbies)
- Vacation & Travel expenses
- Education and training expenses
- Childcare expenses
- Debt repayment (credit cards, loans)
- Miscellaneous expenses (gifts, hobbies, holidays, allowances)

F is for… ***401(k)s, Finances, Foreclosures***

401(k)s are a type of retirement savings plan offered by many employers in the United States. It is named after the section of the Internal Revenue Code that governs it.

401(k) plans allow employees to save a portion of their income for retirement through pre-tax contributions. Employers may also offer matching contributions, further incentivizing employees to save for their future. The funds in a 401(k) account grow tax-free until the employee withdraws the money in retirement, at which point it is taxed as regular income.

401(k) plans typically offer a variety of investment options, including stocks, bonds, and mutual funds. Some plans may also offer additional benefits such as loans and hardship withdrawals.

Personal **Finances** refer to the financial management of an individual's income, expenses, savings, investments, debts, and assets. It involves creating a budget, setting financial goals, managing expenses, tracking income, and making informed decisions about money. Personal finances also include paying bills, saving for emergencies, investing in retirement accounts, and planning for long-term financial security. It is the process of taking control of one's financial situation and making decisions that support financial stability and growth.

Foreclosures are a legal process where a lender takes ownership of a property (such as a primary home or investment property) from a borrower who has defaulted on their mortgage payments. This process is initiated when the borrower has failed to make payments for a specified period of time, typically three to six months. The lender will first send a notice of default to the borrower and may begin the foreclosure process if the payments are not made. The property will then be put up for sale at a public auction, and the proceeds from the sale will go toward paying off the outstanding mortgage balance. If the property is not sold at the auction, the lender may take ownership and try to sell it later. Foreclosures can have a significant impact on the borrower's credit and financial stability and can also affect surrounding property values and the local real estate market.

G is for… ***Grit, Gross Profit/Loss, Growth***

Grit is a term used to describe a person's perseverance and determination in the face of challenges or obstacles. It refers to the ability to stick to one's goals, even in the face of difficulties, and to work hard and persistently to achieve one's objectives. Grit is often seen as a combination of passion, perseverance, and resilience, and is considered an important factor in success and personal growth.

Gross profit/loss is the difference between the revenue and the cost of goods sold in a business. It represents the amount of money a business makes after subtracting the cost of producing the products or services it sells. If the gross profit is positive, it indicates that the business is making a profit from its sales. If the gross profit is negative, it indicates that the business is making a loss and that the cost of goods sold is higher than the revenue generated.

Financial **Growth** refers to an increase in the amount of money, assets, or value of a business, organization, or individual over a period of time. It can be measured by the growth in revenue, profits, net worth, stock price, or other financial metrics. Financial growth is a key indicator of success and stability in the financial sector, and is a goal for many companies and investors. Financial growth can be driven by a variety of factors, such as increased demand for products and services, expanding market share, strategic investments and acquisitions, and effective cost management.

H is for... ***Home buying, Health***

Home buying refers to the process of purchasing a house or other type of property as a permanent residence. It involves various steps, including finding a suitable property, making an offer, negotiating with the seller, securing financing, and completing the necessary paperwork. The process can be complex and may require the assistance of a real estate agent, loan officer, or other professional. Home buying is a significant financial and personal decision, and many factors such as location, budget, and future plans must be considered before making a purchase.

Financial **Health** refers to the overall well-being of an individual's or a company's financial situation. It involves having a balance between income, expenses, savings, and debt, as well as being prepared for future financial challenges. Factors contributing to financial health include having a steady income, managing debt, saving regularly, and investing in a diversified portfolio. Financial health can help individuals and companies achieve financial stability and security, enabling them to reach their financial goals and make informed financial decisions.

I is for... ***IRAs, Income, Inflation, Interest, Investing***

IRAs, or Individual Retirement Accounts, are savings plans that provide tax incentives to encourage individuals to save for their retirement. There are several types of IRAs, including:

1. Traditional IRA: contributions may be tax-deductible, and earnings grow tax-deferred until withdrawal.
2. Roth IRA: contributions are made with after-tax dollars, but withdrawals are tax-free in retirement.
3. SEP IRA: designed for self-employed individuals or small business owners who want to make tax-deferred contributions to their retirement.
4. Simple IRA: Similar to a SEP IRA but designed for small businesses with fewer employees.
5. Rollover IRA: an IRA created when you roll over money from a previous employer's retirement plan into an IRA.

The purpose of IRAs is to help individuals accumulate savings for retirement. IRAs have limits on how much you can contribute each year and may have additional restrictions and penalties for early withdrawals.

Income refers to the amount of money earned by an individual or a business through various sources such as salary, wages, commissions, bonuses, dividends, and rent. It is the total of all sources of revenue received over a specified period of time. In accounting, income is often referred to as "revenue" and is the main component of a company's profits. For individuals, income is used to determine their tax liability and financial stability.

Inflation is an economic phenomenon characterized by a sustained increase in the general price level of goods and services in an economy over a period of time. This leads to a decline in the purchasing power of money, as the same amount of currency can buy fewer goods and services than before. Inflation is caused by a variety of factors, including increased demand for goods and services, changes in the supply and demand of money, and shifts in production costs. Central banks and governments use various tools, such as interest rate adjustments and monetary policy, to manage inflation and keep it within a target range.

Interest is a fee charged by a lender to a borrower for the use of money. It is expressed as a percentage of the amount borrowed and is paid over a set period of time. Interest can be charged on loans, credit cards, savings accounts, and other forms of borrowing or investing. The interest rate is determined by various factors, including the risk of the loan, the current economic conditions, and the length of the loan.

Investing is the act of putting money into stocks, bonds, real estate, or other assets with the expectation of earning a return in the future. The goal of investing is to grow wealth and achieve financial goals, such as retirement planning, wealth preservation, and income generation. Investing involves a degree of risk and requires careful consideration of one's personal financial situation, market conditions, and investment objectives. It involves making informed decisions about the use of funds for the purpose of increasing wealth, generating income, or both.

J is for... ***Job***

A **job** is a paid position of employment within a company or organization. It involves performing specific tasks and duties as agreed upon between the employer and employee, in exchange for compensation such as a salary or hourly wage. Jobs can vary in nature, from manual labor to professional positions, and can be full-time, part-time, or freelance. Jobs are typically a source of income and provide opportunities for growth and development within an industry or field.

K is for... ***Knowledge***

Knowledge is the awareness, understanding, or familiarity with a particular fact, information, or subject. It can refer to the general understanding of a particular field or area of expertise or the specific information gained through education, experience, or observation. Knowledge is the acquisition of information, facts, and skills that are used to understand the world around us and make informed decisions.

L is for… ***Liabilities, Loss***

Liabilities are obligations that arise from the use of borrowed funds or the issuance of financial instruments, such as bonds, loans, and leases. These liabilities require the borrower to repay the debt and make interest payments to the lender. Examples of financial liabilities include loans, mortgages, credit card balances, and other forms of debt. Financial liabilities may also include the obligation to pay for goods and services purchased on credit. These liabilities can negatively impact an individual's credit score and overall financial health if not managed properly.

A financial **loss** is a decrease in an individual or organization's financial assets, income, or value due to factors such as investments that did not perform as expected, expenses that exceeded revenue, or devaluation of assets. It can also refer to a decline in the market value of a stock or bond. Financial losses can have a significant impact on the overall financial stability and future planning of an individual or organization.

M is for… ***Money, Markets***

Money is a medium of exchange and a store of value that is widely recognized and used as a means of payment for goods and services. It provides a common currency that facilitates transactions and eliminates the need for a barter system.

There are various forms of money, including physical currency, such as coins and banknotes, and digital or virtual currency, such as cryptocurrencies. In modern economies, money also refers to bank deposits and other forms of electronic funds transfers. The value of money is based on the trust and confidence people have in it, as well as its scarcity relative to its demand.

Financial **markets** are platforms where participants can buy and sell financial instruments such as stocks, bonds, currencies, commodities, and derivatives. These markets provide a way for companies and governments to raise capital and for investors to access investment opportunities. They are characterized by the presence of intermediaries such as brokers and exchanges, and by the use of market-determined prices to reflect the supply and demand for the financial instruments being traded. Financial markets play a critical role in the functioning of modern economies and are essential for the allocation of capital to its most productive uses. Examples of financial markets include the stock market, bond market, currency market, commodity market, and derivatives market.

N is for...***Needs, Net Profit/Loss, Net Worth***

Financial **needs** refers to the funds or resources required to meet various expenses, such as living costs, bills, loans, investments, savings, and unexpected emergencies. These needs vary from person to person based on income, lifestyle, age, family size, and future goals. These needs can be met through different financial strategies, such as budgeting, saving, investing, and borrowing. It is important to have a balanced approach to meeting financial needs, balancing spending, and saving for both present and future expenses.

Net profit/loss is the difference between revenue and expenses for a business or an individual. It is the amount that remains after all costs, including operating expenses and taxes, have been subtracted from total income. If the net profit/loss is positive, the business or individual has made a profit. If the net profit/loss is negative, the business or individual has sustained a loss.

Net worth is the total value of a person's assets minus their liabilities. It represents the estimated amount of money a person would have left over if they sold all their assets and paid off all their debts. This includes real estate, investments, personal property, and cash savings. Net worth is often used to measure a person's financial well-being and stability.

O is for... ***Opportunities, Outstanding Bills, Owner's Equity***

Opportunities refer to favorable circumstances, conditions, or chances that allow an individual or organization to achieve a desired goal or objective. Opportunities can be found in various areas, including business, career, education, personal growth, and more. They can take the form of new markets, untapped customer segments, innovative technologies, shifts in consumer behavior, and other factors. Some common examples of opportunities include:

- Starting a new business
- Pursuing a new career path
- Investing in stocks, real estate, or other assets
- Gaining new skills or knowledge through education and training
- Traveling to new places and experiencing different cultures

The ability to recognize and capitalize on opportunities is often seen as a key factor in personal and professional success. It requires a combination of creativity, vision, risk-taking, and strategic thinking. By staying aware of environmental changes and being open to new possibilities, individuals and organizations can create new opportunities for themselves and others.

Outstanding bills refer to any unpaid bills or debts that have yet to be settled. These include utilities, credit card bills, rent or mortgage payments, insurance premiums, medical bills, loan repayments, and other financial obligations. They are considered outstanding because they have not been paid or settled, and the due date has passed.

Owner's Equity is the portion of a company's total assets that is owned by its shareholders or proprietor. It represents the residual interest in the assets of a business after deducting liabilities. It is also called shareholders' equity, net worth, or simply equity. The formula for owner's equity is:

Owner's Equity = Assets - Liabilities

In other words, it is the amount of money that would be left over if all of a company's assets were sold and all its debts were paid off.

P is for… ***Profit, Payday***

Profit describes the financial benefit realized when the revenue generated from a business activity exceeds the expenses, costs, and taxes involved in sustaining the activity in question.

There are three main types of profit: gross, operating, and net.

- *Gross profit* shows the money left after paying for the goods and services sold.
- *Operating profit* shows what's left after paying operating costs such as rent, electricity, phones, and payroll.
- *Net profit* shows what you made after deducting all costs, including taxes. Net profit is what is available for the owners and shareholders.

A **payday** is a specific day of the month when an employee receives their salary or wage payment for the work they have performed. It is usually a set date, and the amount paid will depend on the number of hours worked, overtime, bonuses, etc. Paydays can be daily, weekly, bi-weekly, bi-monthly, or monthly.

Q is for… ***Qualified retirement plan***

A **Qualified Retirement Plan** is a plan established by an employer for its employees that meets the requirements of Internal Revenue Code Section 401(a) or 403(a) and is eligible for special tax considerations. The plan may provide for employer contributions, as in a pension or profit-sharing plan, and employee contributions. Employers can deduct plan contributions made on behalf of eligible employees on the business's tax return as business expenses. Plan earnings are not taxed to the employee until withdrawn.

R is for… ***Rent, Retirement, Return on Investment, Risk***

Rent is a regular payment made by a tenant to a landlord for the use of a property, such as a house, apartment, or commercial space. The payment is typically made on a monthly or yearly basis and provides the tenant with the right to live or work in the property for a specified period of time.

Retirement is the process of leaving one's job, either because of reaching a certain age or due to personal circumstances, with the intention of no longer working for an employer. Retirement usually marks the end of a person's career and is considered a major life event. It typically involves transitioning to a new lifestyle and beginning to rely on savings, investments, and other sources of income to support one in one's post-work years.

Return on Investment (ROI) is a financial metric used to evaluate the profitability of an investment. It is a ratio that compares the net profit or loss generated by an investment to the amount of money invested. ROI is expressed as a percentage and is calculated as follows:

ROI = (Net Profit / Cost of Investment) x 100

The net profit is the difference between the total revenue generated by the investment and the total cost of the investment. The cost of investment includes all expenses incurred to acquire and maintain the investment, such as the purchase price, transaction fees, and ongoing expenses.

ROI is commonly used by investors to compare the potential returns of different investments and to make decisions about which investments to pursue. A higher ROI indicates a more profitable investment, while a lower ROI indicates a less profitable investment. It is important to note that ROI does not consider the time value of money or the risks associated with an investment. Therefore, it should be used in conjunction with other financial metrics to make informed investment decisions.

Financial **risk** refers to the uncertainty associated with the future outcome of an investment or financial decision. It is the potential loss or decrease in value that a person or organization may face due to changes in market conditions, economic factors, or other unpredictable events. Financial risk can arise from various sources, such as credit risk, market risk, operational risk, and currency risk. To manage financial risk, investors and organizations typically use a variety of strategies, including diversification, hedging, and risk mitigation techniques.

S is for… ***Sales, Savings, Spending, Stocks***

Sales refers to persuading or encouraging a customer to buy a product or service. It is the process of identifying, attracting, and engaging potential customers and ultimately converting them into paying clients. Sales encompasses various stages, from lead generation and qualification to product presentation, closing, and post-sales follow-up. Sales is an essential aspect of a business's success and helps drive revenue and growth.

Savings refers to the amount of money that a person or organization has set aside or not spent, usually for the purpose of future spending or investment. It is the amount of money left after all expenses and debts have been paid. Savings can be used for emergency situations, long-term investments, retirement funds, or other financial goals.

Spending refers to using money to purchase goods, services, or experiences. It can be done by individuals, households, businesses, and governments. Spending is an important aspect of personal finance and economic activity as it drives demand and contributes to growth in the economy.

Stocks are units of ownership in a company that are publicly traded on stock exchanges. When you buy a stock, you own a small piece of the company and have the right to vote on certain decisions, and receive a portion of the company's profits in the form of dividends. The price of a stock can fluctuate based on market demand and various other factors. Investors buy stocks with the hope of making a profit through either price appreciation or dividend payments.

T is for… ***Taxes, Trusts***

Taxes are fees imposed by the government on the income, goods, services, or property of individuals and businesses. The purpose of taxes is to generate revenue for the government to fund public services and programs. Taxes can be in the form of income tax, sales tax, property tax, etc. Taxes are typically calculated based on the individual's or business's financial situation and are required to be paid annually or periodically. Failure to pay taxes can result in penalties, fines, or legal consequences.

A **trust** is a legal arrangement in which one or more parties, known as the trustor, transfers assets to another party, known as the trustee, to be held and managed for the benefit of a third party, known as the beneficiary. The trustee is responsible for managing and investing the assets in accordance with the terms of the trust agreement and for distributing the assets to the beneficiary in accordance with the agreement. Trusts can be established for various purposes, including protecting assets, managing and preserving assets for future generations, managing assets for someone unable to do so, or providing for a specific purpose or charitable cause.

U is for... ***Unemployment***

Unemployment refers to a situation in which individuals who are willing and able to work cannot find employment. This can be due to a number of factors, such as economic downturns, lack of job opportunities, or mismatch between skills and job requirements. Unemployment can have a significant impact on the economy, as well as on the affected individuals and their families, in terms of reduced income and spending power.

V is for... ***Value, Volatility***

Value refers to the worth or usefulness of something, determined by its perceived benefits, scarcity, and the satisfaction it provides. It can refer to the monetary price of an item or to the intrinsic value that it holds for an individual or a society. It is a subjective concept that can vary from person to person, depending on their needs, beliefs, and cultural background.

Volatility is the degree of price variation or price fluctuations of a security, currency, or market index over time. It measures the rate at which the price of a financial instrument changes over time, usually expressed as a percentage. High volatility means that the price of a financial instrument is rapidly changing, while low volatility indicates that the price changes more slowly or steadily. Volatility is an important factor for traders and investors, as it affects the level of risk involved in financial investment.

W is for… ***Wall Street, Wants, Wealth, Will***

Wall Street is a street located in the Financial District of Lower Manhattan in New York City, USA. It is the historic home of the New York Stock Exchange (NYSE) and serves as the financial center of the United States.

The term "Wall Street" is often used colloquially to refer to the financial industry, particularly the stock market, investment banks, and other financial institutions that operate in the area. It is a hub of financial activity, where many of the world's largest corporations, banks, and financial services companies are headquartered. It has also become synonymous with high-powered financial deals, risk-taking, and wealth creation.

Wants are desires or aspirations that individuals or groups of people have and seek to fulfill. They are often seen as the things that people would like to have or experience but are not necessarily essential for their survival or well-being. Wants can be material or non-material and can vary depending on factors such as personal preferences, cultural norms, economic status, and social influences. For example, some common wants may include things like a new car, a bigger house, a vacation, or the latest electronic gadgets, while others may include more intangible things like love, respect, or happiness.

Wealth can be defined as the abundance of valuable possessions or resources, often expressed in terms of monetary value. These possessions and resources can include money, property, investments, assets, and other tangible or intangible items with value.

Wealth can also refer to a person's overall financial and economic status, including income, assets, debts, and financial stability. It is often measured in terms of net worth, which is the value of a person's assets minus their liabilities.

While wealth is often associated with financial success, it is important to note that it is not the only indicator of success or happiness. Many prioritize other factors, such as relationships, health, and personal fulfillment, over accumulating wealth.

A **will** is a legal document that outlines how a person's assets and property should be distributed after their death. It is also known as a last will and testament. The document usually includes the name of the person creating the will (the testator), the beneficiaries who will receive the assets, and the executor who will be responsible for carrying out the instructions in the will.

A will can also include other important information such as funeral arrangements, guardianship of minor children, and instructions for distributing personal property. A will can be updated or changed at any time during the testator's lifetime, as long as they are mentally competent and follow the legal procedures for making changes to a will.

It is important to have a will in place to ensure that your wishes are carried out after your death and to prevent disputes among family members. Without a will, the distribution of assets and property will be determined by the laws of the state where the person lived, which may not reflect their true intentions.

X is for... ***Xenocurrency***

The term **Xenocurrency** refers to any currency that is traded in markets outside of its domestic borders. Its name derives from the Greek prefix "xeno," meaning "foreign."

Today, the use of the term xenocurrency is infrequent as the prefix xeno can have negative connotations in modern English. Xenophobia, for example, means an irrational fear of or hatred toward foreigners. *Foreign currency*, therefore, has become the preferred term for referring to non-domestic currencies.

Y is for... ***Yield***

In financial terms, **Yield** refers to the return on investment an investor receives on a particular security, such as stocks, bonds, or mutual funds. Yield is expressed as a percentage and can be calculated differently depending on the type of security being evaluated.

For example, in the case of a bond, yield represents the interest paid by the issuer to the bondholder over the life of the bond and is calculated by dividing the annual interest payments by the bond's current market price. This is known as the current yield.

In the case of stocks, yield refers to the dividends paid by the company to its shareholders and is calculated by dividing the annual dividends per share by the stock's current market price. This is known as the dividend yield.

Yield is an important measure for investors, as it provides an indication of the potential return on investment, which helps investors to make informed decisions about whether to buy or sell a particular security.

Z is for… ***Zero-balance budget***

A **Zero-Balance Budget** is a budgeting system in which you allocate every dollar of your income toward a specific expense or savings goal, with the end result being that your income minus your expenses and savings equals zero. This means you have accounted for every dollar you have earned and allocated it toward a specific purpose, rather than letting any funds go unaccounted for or sit idly in your bank account.

With a zero-balance budget, you start by identifying your income and then create a plan for how you will spend or save each dollar. You may need to prioritize your spending and make trade-offs to ensure that you can cover all your essential expenses and savings goals. The goal of a zero-balance budget is to help you track your spending and ensure that you are not overspending or underspending in any category.

Overall, a zero-balance budget can be a useful tool for managing your finances, as it forces you to be intentional and proactive with your money while ensuring you are not wasting any resources.

While these are just a few key principles for you to begin your financial journey, I hope it has whetted your appetite to learn more. There are many great books on finance and investing. I have listed them at the back of the book. I have read and found great value in every book I recommend. The more you know, the more confident you will be.

BOOK RECOMMENDATIONS

The Truth About Money by Ric Edelman

ACTION MAP

1. Work through all the exercises for this chapter in the *Go For It!* Companion Workbook
2. Reflect on how you want to build a stronger financial foundation to achieve your dreams.
3. Read *The Truth About Money*

Bonus story that illustrates my story at the beginning of the chapter.

An Airbus 380 is on its way across the Atlantic. It flies consistently at 800 km/h at 30,000 feet when suddenly a Eurofighter with a Tempo Mach 2 appears.

The pilot of the fighter jet slows down, flies alongside the Airbus and greets the pilot of the passenger plane by radio: "Airbus, boring flight, isn't it? Now, have a look here!"

He rolls his jet on its back, accelerates, breaks through the sound barrier, rises rapidly to a dizzying height, and then swoops down almost to sea level in a breathtaking dive. He loops back next to the Airbus and asks: "Well, how was that?"

The Airbus pilot answers: "Very impressive, but watch this!"

The jet pilot watches the Airbus, but nothing happens. It continues to fly straight at the same speed. After 15 minutes, the Airbus pilot radios, "Well, how was that?"

Confused, the jet pilot asks, "What did you do?"

The Airbus pilot laughs and says: "I got up, stretched my legs, walked to the back of the aircraft to use the washroom, then got a cup of coffee and a chocolate fudge pastry."

The story's moral is: When you're young, speed and adrenaline seem great. But as you get older and wiser, you learn that comfort and peace are more important.

This is called S.O.S.: *Slower, Older,* and *Smarter*. It's time to slow down and enjoy the rest of the trip.

(Author Unknown)

CHAPTER EIGHT

Interest Never Sleeps

"Compound interest is the eighth wonder of the world. He who understands it, earns it. He who doesn't... pays it."
— Albert Einstein

My husband and I started the practice when we first got married that Christmas would always be debt-free. We have a Christmas savings account where a portion of our paychecks goes into each payday. As the account builds up, we can buy things throughout the year when they are on sale. Paying cash for Christmas means there is never stress come January. My husband is also good about making extra payments on our car loans and mortgage, so we don't have a payment due in December, which gives us even more spending cash that month. He pays the monthly payment plus 1/11th of a payment each month from January to November.

Disclaimer: You need to see if your loan is set up to do so before making the extra payments.

We LOVE to travel. We love exploring new places, trying new foods (well, my family does), and seeing the incredible beauty of this world. A Christmas tradition we added several years ago is taking a major trip over the Christmas/New Year holidays every other year. The year we are taking the trip, we don't celebrate with presents. The trip *is* the present to the family. We have traveled all over the world. We have created experiences and memories no toy could ever provide. We have ziplined in Jamaica, Hawaii, and St. Thomas. We have parasailed in St. Kitts, Grand Cayman, and Key West. We have helicoptered over the island of Oahu. We love to do lots of things on our vacations, and they cost money.

The number one rule of our trips is that they are paid for upfront in cash. We save for two years, so there are never any regrets after a trip. There is no worse feeling than going on an incredible trip, then dreading opening the credit card bill for months, or even years, making payments for something long over. We know how powerful interest can be, and we have found it's a lot more fun earning it than paying it.

WHEN COMPOUND INTEREST WORKS FOR YOU

Compound interest is one of the most powerful financial concepts that exists. It is the process of earning interest on the initial principal amount as well as on the accumulated interest over time. This means that the interest earned in one period is added to the principal, and the interest is then calculated on the new, higher amount. Over time, this compounding effect can lead to significant growth in wealth.

To understand the power of compounding interest, let's consider an example. Suppose you invest $10,000 in a savings account that earns an annual interest rate of 5%, compounded monthly. After one year, your investment would be worth $10,511.62. However, if you continued to leave your investment in the account and let it compound for 10 years, your investment would be worth $16,386.87. That's an increase of over 60% from the initial investment amount.

The longer you leave your money invested, the more powerful the compounding effects become. For example, if you left your investment in the account for 30 years, your investment would be worth $43,219.17. That's more than four times the initial investment amount!

The power of compounding interest can also be seen in the stock market. Suppose you invest $10,000 in a stock with an average annual return of 10%. If you reinvest all your dividends and leave your investment to compound for 30 years, your investment would be worth $174,494.72. That's an increase of almost 1,650% from the initial investment amount.

One of the key factors that determine the power of compounding interest is time. The longer you leave your money invested, the more time it has to compound, and the more your investment will grow. This means saving early is crucial if you want to benefit from the power of compounding interest.

Another important factor is the interest rate. A higher interest rate will lead to faster growth, while a lower interest rate will lead to slower growth. This is why it's important to shop around for the best interest rates when choosing a savings account or other investment.

The power of compounding interest is an incredibly powerful financial concept that can lead to significant growth in wealth over time. By starting to save early, choosing the right investments, and letting your money compound over a long period, you can maximize the benefits of compounding interest and achieving your financial goals.

WHEN COMPOUND INTEREST WORKS AGAINST YOU

Compounding interest is a double-edged sword, though. Just as you saw how powerful it is working for you, it is just as aggressive at working against you if you are not financially savvy. Compounding interest can also work against individuals who have debt, causing them to pay much more than the initial amount borrowed.

When an individual borrows money, they are often required to pay back the borrowed amount plus interest. The interest rate is the percentage of the borrowed amount that must be paid back as a fee for borrowing the money. If the interest rate is compounded, the interest is calculated on the principal amount plus any interest already accrued. This means that the interest owed on the debt grows over time, even if the individual is only making minimum payments.

For example, consider a credit card debt of $5,000 with an annual interest rate of 20%. If the individual only makes minimum payments of 2% of the balance each month, it will take them over 30 years to pay off the debt, and they will end up paying over $16,000 in interest alone. This is because the interest is compounding each month, and the interest owed on the debt grows larger and larger over time.

The longer an individual carries debt with compounding interest, the more they will end up paying in interest fees. This is especially true for high-interest debt like credit card debt, which can have interest rates as high as 30% or more. Even a small balance can quickly grow into a large debt if left unpaid over time.

Compounding interest can also work against individuals who have taken out loans like mortgages or car loans. These loans often have long repayment terms, meaning the interest has more time to compound. This can result in the individual paying much more than the initial amount borrowed over the life of the loan.

The power of compounding interest can work for or against individuals depending on their financial situation. While compounding interest can help individuals accumulate wealth over time, it can also lead to significant debt if not managed carefully. It is important to be mindful of the interest rates and repayment terms of any loans or debts to avoid being caught in a cycle of debt with compounding interest working against you.

Learning to wait for what you want is an important lesson to becoming financially savvy and financially free.

RESOURCES

The Power of Zero Documentary

BOOK RECOMMENDATIONS

Rich Dad Poor Dad by Robert Kiyosaki

ACTION MAP

1. Work through all the exercises for this chapter in the *Go For It!* Companion Workbook
2. Look at ways to eliminate the interest you are paying
3. Look at ways to earn more interest on your investments
4. Schedule a free, no-obligation appointment to review your retirement & investing strategies at https://calendly.com/lifeonpurposeacademyut/clarity
5. Read *Rich Dad Poor Dad*

CHAPTER NINE

How to Invest in Your Future

"It's not how much money you make, but how much money you keep, how hard it works for you, and how many generations you keep it for."
— Robert Kiyosaki

Remember the VW diesel Rabbit? Well, it was the 80s, and we were complaining that diesel fuel was up to 99 cents. I know, right?!?! But it was a big deal at the time. There was an oil crisis in Iran, and people were lined up for blocks at gas stations trying to fill up because there was a threat there would be no more fuel for a while. Crazy times. Because we lived near the Mexican border, we drove to Tijuana every Sunday to get diesel and have tacos for lunch. We had a nice day, saved 20 cents on fuel and thought we were pretty smart.

In reality, it was a false economy. We paid more for the diesel once we purchased the additive to the tank because it was a lesser-grade diesel. It took way more time than sitting in line at the gas station, especially with the lines trying to come back across the border into the States. But it gave us something to do and made for some funny memories.

When I was a teenager, my sister and I would leave San Diego and spend four to six weeks in Oregon with my grandparents every summer. My parents weren't there, it was just my sister and me. We had so much fun with our grandparents. My grandfather came from a large family. He was the third of nine children. He was born in 1911. He told great "I remember when" stories – like growing up using the Sears catalog as toilet paper. He was a logger when he was younger and a real estate broker later on in life. If you ever go to North Bend, OR, there is a cute logging museum on the main Highway 101 next to Simpson Park. Much of the logging memorabilia came from my grandfather, Warren Dick.

I bring my grandfather up because of my memories of him watching the stock market when we were there each summer. At the time, he was in his seventies, and I loved his predictable life. He was one of those early-to-bed, early-to-rise people. He'd wake up before the sun, read the paper, have a hearty breakfast, watch the stock market, and then work in his garden or woodshop for a while. He'd then come in to watch the stock market for a few minutes mid-morning and return to his garden or the shop. He'd then come in, get cleaned up for lunch, and put on his "good shirt" because we were "going into town" for lunch.

His favorite restaurant was The King's Table. It was one of those all-you-can-eat buffets with the BEST fried chicken and desserts. Everything a teenager wants! We rarely went out to eat at home, so going out to eat almost every day was a huge treat for us. Everyone there knew him, and I can't remember a time when someone didn't stop by our table to say hello, tell us how much we had grown since they saw us the year before, and swap some gossip.

After lunch, we'd go back home, where he'd check the stock market again, change into his work clothes, and return to the woodshop for a few hours. He did woodworking, and I loved being out in his big shop with the smell of sawdust and the sound of power tools. Once more, he'd trek back into the house to watch the stock market at the end of the day. We'd then go out to the garden, pick some fresh veggies to sell at the local fruit stand, and bring in a few more items from the garden to eat for dinner. We'd talk all night about the "good old days," and then he'd go to bed early and do it all over again the next day. I loved it!!!

At my age, I didn't understand the stock market. I didn't know why my grandfather came in multiple times a day to watch the TV for a few minutes, make a call occasionally, and then go about his day. I just knew what I was told — that my grandfather was "good with his money."

As I got older and got married, I didn't see my grandfather as often. I later came to learn that my grandfather's trusted stockbroker retired, and he was appointed a new one. The new one was younger and apparently talked my grandfather into investing in some riskier stocks, where my grandfather lost almost everything. It broke my heart to see my grandfather lose almost everything he had in his 80s after working so hard all of his life. That is when I began to put up blocks and detest the stock market.

My grandfather's story wasn't the first, nor the last, that I heard about people losing everything "in the market."

My sweet father-in-law invested in the market as well when he was alive. We teased him constantly because he liked to "buy high and sell low." It was a running joke in the family that he kept losing in the market, but it didn't deter him from trying. We may have teased him, but seeing the losses always made me sad. Again, it reiterated why I hated the market. The people I loved were always losing money.

Later, when I returned to school, I took a finance class where we had a module on investing, and I HATED it. I hated even the idea of using fake money to purchase a stock I had analyzed and decided to invest in and follow. I hated the idea of tracking my money going up and down, and I resented being asked to do something I hated so much. So, I flat-out didn't. I didn't do one assignment in that module. Ultimately, I had to write a paper on what we learned. I did, in fact, write *that* paper. In it, I was a tad vehement about my opinion of the market, why I thought it was horrible, how it hurt people, yada yada yada. I got an A on the paper, and my professor wrote in his feedback to me that he would hate to know what I *really* thought about investing.

I laugh at that situation now as I am a financial advisor who works with people to make money in and out of the stock market. It's funny how time and some real-life education can create a change of mind and heart. It almost makes me want to write and tell my professor about it. *Almost.*

Warren Buffet says, "Never depend on a single income; make investments to create a second source."

As I mentioned, overcoming my fear of the market took me years. I'm embarrassed to say just how many years it took. But now, we have multiple strategies to make our money work for us – the market being one of them.

The key to my change of heart was education. As the saying goes, "Knowledge is power." In this chapter, I want to give you the power that comes with knowledge on how to design your retirement and investments to fit YOUR needs strategically.

I want to build a foundation and understanding of the importance of building a retirement plan for your future… NOW! It doesn't matter how old you are at this moment. Today is the day to be thinking of your future.

When I meet with clients, I know that their financial situation is as unique as they are. I believe there are times to take advantage of the market and times to protect clients' investments. And as we all know, investors' emotions and short-term behaviors can influence their long-term financial goals.

- We live in a wealthy and highly educated country, and yet…
- The median household income reported by retired Americans in 2020 is only $43,696.
- (*Boston College Center for Retirement Research*)
- The average 50-year-old has less than $50,000 saved for retirement. (*2017 US Census Bureau*)
- 50% of households are at major risk of not accumulating enough to maintain their lifestyle in retirement. (*Boston College Center for Retirement Research*)
- Only 4% of Americans have achieved financial independence!

Those are some staggering and sobering statistics. That means only 4% of people can support themselves without government help (Social Security, Medicaid, etc.) in their retirement years. That is a LOT of people who will need help and need to rely on others to survive. I don't know about you, but I don't want to be in a position where I must rely on the government for anything.

There are plenty of people in retirement who desire to be social, give back, and stay active. They volunteer, get a part-time job, and they have hobbies that keep them busy. I joke with clients that I want them to work at Walmart during retirement because they WANT to, not because they HAVE to!

So, let's discuss why the best time to invest is NOW! If you are young and have plenty of years to invest, you will be in great shape… if you do it! If you are older, I want to give you hope that there is still time! As mentioned earlier, my husband and I lost everything in my late 30s and his early 40s. We spent another ten years stumbling along trying to figure things out, and now in our 50s, we have a multiple-prong approach to our retirement plan that will set us up to retire comfortably without having to wait until our 80s to do so!

TIME

Time is the great equalizer of life. Understanding the importance of leveraging time for your present and future needs is the greatest tool in your tool belt. In investing, timing is EVERYTHING. The image below is the perfect example of why starting as early as possible makes such a big difference. These numbers are based on a 10% annual return. Just take a look at the difference starting early can make! The magic of investing is compound interest. Remember in chapter 11 when we discussed how interest is always working for or against you? Well, this is the perfect example of compounding interest working *for* you.

TIME IS MONEY

MR. START EARLY

26	$6,000	43	0	56	0
27	$6,000	44	0	57	0
28	$6,000	45	0	58	0
29	$6,000	46	0	59	0
30	$6,000	47	0	60	0
31	$6,000	48	0	61	0
32	$6,000	49	0	62	0
33	$6,000	50	0	63	0
34	$6,000	51	0	64	0
35	$6,000	52	0	65	0
36	0	53	0		
37	0	54	0		
38	0	55	0		
39	0				
40	0				
41	0				
42	0				

TOTAL CONTRIBUTION: $60,000
AT AGE 65: $2,031,722

10% return

MR. WAIT LONGER

26	0	43	$6,000	56	$6,000
27	0	44	$6,000	57	$6,000
28	0	45	$6,000	58	$6,000
29	0	46	$6,000	59	$6,000
30	0	47	$6,000	60	$6,000
31	0	48	$6,000	61	$6,000
32	0	49	$6,000	62	$6,000
33	0	50	$6,000	63	$6,000
34	0	51	$6,000	64	$6,000
35	0	52	$6,000	65	$6,000
36	$6,000	53	$6,000		
37	$6,000	54	$6,000		
38	$6,000	55	$6,000		
39	$6,000				
40	$6,000				
41	$6,000				
42	$6,000				

TOTAL CONTRIBUTION: $180,000
AT AGE 65: $1,130,243

Mr. Start Early starts investing $500 per month at the age of 26, which still isn't *that* early. He invests $6,000 per year for 10 years and never again adds to his investment. Just by making that initial investment for ten years at an earlier age, he is able to grow his $60,000 investment to a whopping $2 million.

That is the power of compound interest. You earn interest on the money you originally save plus on the interest you've accumulated. As your investments grow, you earn interest on a larger and larger pool of money. Mr. Early contributed one-third the amount of Mr. Wait Longer and earned twice as much!

Compound interest is the secret to building wealth. It is one of the most basic principles of investing. If you want to build wealth, you must quit *paying* interest (debt) and start *earning* interest (investing). Just like we talked about buying low and selling high in the market, we want to earn interest, not pay it.

We know that time is our friend when it comes to investing. The more time we have to let our money grow, the better. You may think you're in trouble if you are older and don't have as much time. I feel you. I was there! Because of the poor decisions I made earlier in life, I had nothing and had to start over in my mid-forties. That is even later than Mr. Wait Longer… by a DECADE! But I'm here to tell you there is hope! There are strategies that can still give you a great return, even if you are starting later in life.

Time is the number one factor in earning wealth. Time is forgiving and can make up for losses. If you look at a graph of your investments, you will see many peaks and dips. If you look at a very short period of time, say one month, there may be a huge dip that might scare you. However, if you zoom out and look at a 20-year period, you might see that even though there was a dip during that month, you still had a good run and see that your money increased over time. That is why making investing and financial decisions without emotion is important. You may see a huge dip in one month, panic, pull everything out, and take a huge loss, whereas had you not reacted, you would have benefited from a rebound and continued to make a lot of money over the years. We will talk later about how to set parameters for your investing strategies to take the emotions out of investing.

GOOD RETURNS

If time is the number one factor in wealth, good returns are a very close second. You want your money to work for you. You work hard for your money and should want your money to work hard for you. You want your money to grow as quickly as possible, so your returns matter. You have one goal when you invest – to make money! And you should want to make as much money as possible.

Four percent. It sure doesn't sound like a lot. It especially doesn't sound like it could do much damage to your money when you're investing. But let's look at the difference between earning six percent on your investment and earning ten percent over time. Mr. Early decided to invest $500 each month for 40 years. He made good investments and earned 10% each year on his investment, earning a total of $3,162,040! That is a great return on a $240,000 investment! What happens though, if Mr. Early isn't careful and thinks that four percent won't make that much difference and just earns six percent over the years? At six percent, Mr. Early only earns $995,745. That's over a $2 million difference!

How would you like to miss out on $2 million? I know I wouldn't! Mr. Early worked hard for that $240,000 investment, and I know you work hard for your money. For the same investment, you should want your money to work harder and smarter on your behalf.

You may think there is no way to earn that kind of investment year after year. I'm here to tell you that plenty of investment strategies can earn you 10% each and every year.

TAXES

As a financial advisor, I want to help you pay as little of your hard-earned money in taxes as possible. I don't know about you, but I sure as heck don't want to spend 40 years saving my money only to have Uncle Sam take half of it at the end when I actually need it to live off of for the rest of my life! What is the point of strategizing and worrying for 40 years to ensure you earn enough for retirement only to have a large portion of it taken away?

In his book, *The Power of Zero*, David McKnight shows us why investing strategically is so important to pay the least taxes possible in retirement. There are three main ways to invest your money, and I want to review each of them with you and show you the tax implications for each one on the earnings/interest you accrue.

Taxed Annually

Short-term capital investments are taxed as though they are ordinary income. When you sell a capital asset for more than its original price, the result is a capital gain. Capital assets include stocks, bonds, precious metals, jewelry, and real estate. Selling a capital asset after owning it for less than a year results in a short-term capital gain, which is taxed as ordinary income. Day trading is a prime example of short-term capital investing and will be taxed annually. Your profits are taxable as ordinary income and can be taxed up to 37%**, depending on your tax bracket. Capital gains tax on gains related to art, antiques, jewelry, precious metals, stamp collections, coins, and other collectibles is a flat 28% regardless of your income.

Tax Deferred

We've all heard of different tax strategies with tax-deferred options like employer-sponsored retirement plans such as 401(k), 403(b), or 457, allowing both the employer and the employee to make pre-tax contributions. Many employers offer a matching contribution in these types of accounts, making them attractive to employees. Free money!

There are also individual retirement accounts (IRAs). IRAs can be either Traditional or Roth. Traditional IRAs allow you to contribute on a pre-tax basis, depending on your income level and some other factors. With a Roth IRA, you make post-tax contributions, meaning earnings could be tax-free if certain conditions are met.

These plans are established to help you to save on taxes now. But eventually, you do have to pay Uncle Sam. You will be taxed on your contributions and earnings when you pull your money out at retirement. The hard pill to swallow here is that you don't know the tax rate when you are ready to retire. Yikes!

You're taking a small tax break now to pay more taxes in retirement. That doesn't seem like a good plan to me. Hold on! I'm not saying don't take advantage of them; I'm saying that you should be very strategic in using these accounts. Did you know that you can actually overfund your 401k and

Traditional IRA? You can, and no one seems to be helping people understand this.

When you retire and start pulling money out of your 401(k) or Traditional IRA, there is a minimum distribution amount you must pull from your account each year of 4%. Depending on how much is in your account, that 4% draw could increase your taxable income and push you over the threshold where your Social Security benefits are now taxable. It can also make your account dwindle faster than you had hoped.

If you are an individual and your combined income from wages, self-employment, interest, dividends, and other taxable income totals between $25,000 and $34,000, you may have to pay income tax on up to 50% of your social security benefit. If your combined income is over $34,000, you may be required to pay tax on up to 85% of your benefit.

Tax-Free

Looking at this chart, it is easy to see why we want to make sure that we are careful in deciding which investment strategies we choose because they significantly impact how much of our hard-earned money we get to keep. Using the same $3 million Mr. Early worked hard to save over 40 years, we can see how the growth of his money will be taxed.

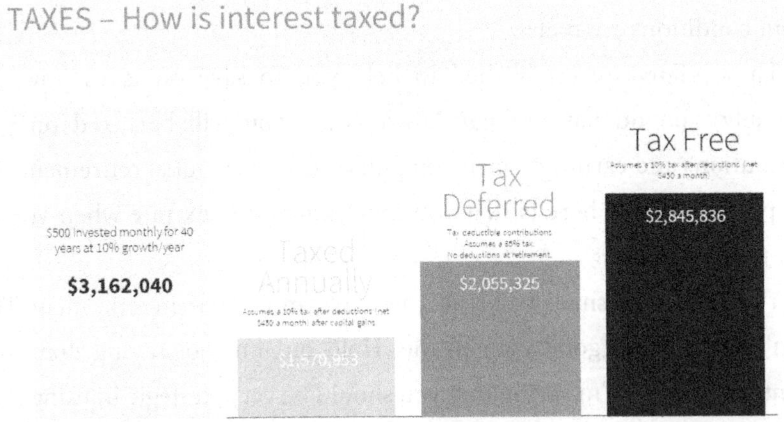

INVESTMENT STRATEGIES

Warren Buffet says, "The poor are poor because they spend all of their money. The middle class are middle class because they save all their money. The wealthy are wealthy because they invest all of their money."

The image below shows the most common ways people invest their money.

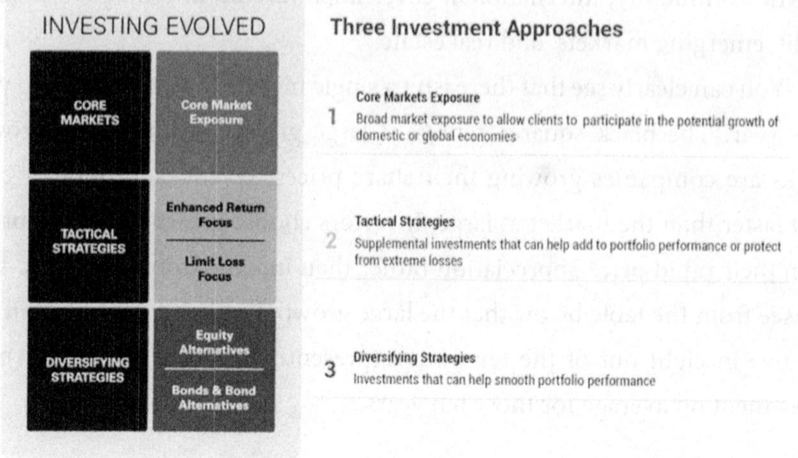

1. **Core Markets.** Core market exposure is investing directly in the stock market. The upside is you get to gain all of the upsides of the market. The downside is you also reap all of the losses in the market.
2. **Tactical Strategies.** This is investing in indexed markets. Indexed markets follow the stock market but protect you from extreme losses. They can do this because they also limit the upside of the market. This may seem unfair at first glance, but there is a great benefit to only seeing most of the upside to limit or even eliminate your losses.
3. **Diversifying Strategies.** Diversification can help manage risk. To build a diversified portfolio, you should look for investments whose returns haven't historically moved in the same direction and to the same degree. The idea is that even if a portion of your portfolio is

declining, the rest of your portfolio is more likely to be growing or at least not declining as much.

This next table is a little "loud," I know. It's also very hard to read, and that's okay. It still provides a great visual representation of the different markets' performance from 2010 through 2019. These markets include small value, small growth, mid value, mid growth, large value, large core, large growth, commodity, international, government/credit, interim government/credit, emerging markets, and real estate.

You can clearly see that there isn't a single market that stayed on top year after year. The black squares represent large growth stocks. Large growth stocks are companies growing their share prices, revenues, profits, or cash flow faster than the market at large. Investors choose growth stocks to profit from their rapid price appreciation rather than income from dividends. You can see from the table below that the large growth market did perform in the top five in eight out of the ten years represented and was the top earning investment on average for those ten years.

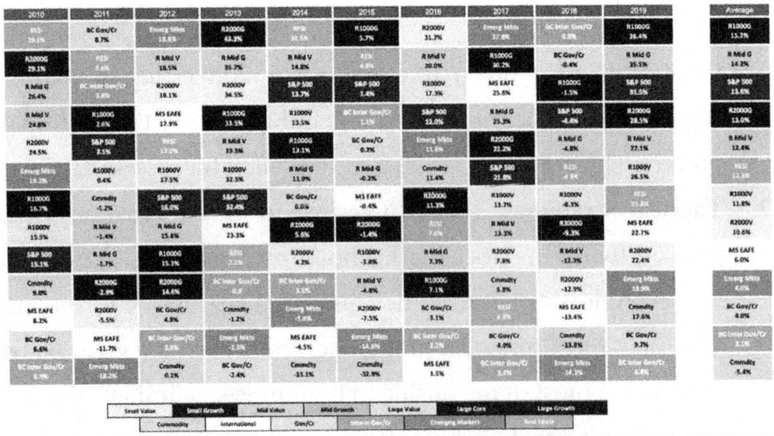

2010	2011	2012	2013	2014	2015	2016	2017	2018	2019	Average
RESI [illegible]	BC Gov/Cr 8.7%	Emerg Mkts [illegible]	R2000G 43.3%	RESI [illegible]	R1000G 5.7%	R2000V 31.7%	Emerg Mkts 37.8%	BC Inter Gov/Cr 0.9%	R1000G 36.4%	R1000G 15.2%
R2000G 29.1%	RESI [illegible]	R Mid V 18.5%	R Mid G 35.7%	R Mid V 14.8%	RESI [illegible]	R Mid V 20.0%	R1000G 30.2%	BC Gov/Cr -0.4%	R Mid G 35.5%	R Mid G 14.2%
R Mid G 26.4%	BC Inter Gov/Cr [illegible]	R2000V 18.1%	R2000V 34.5%	S&P 500 13.7%	S&P 500 1.4%	R1000V 17.3%	MS EAFE 25.8%	R1000G -1.5%	S&P 500 31.5%	S&P 500 13.6%
R Mid V 24.8%	R1000G 2.6%	MS EAFE 17.9%	R1000G 33.5%	R1000V 13.5%	BC Inter Gov/Cr 1.1%	S&P 500 12.0%	R Mid G 25.3%	S&P 500 -4.4%	R2000G 28.5%	R2000G 13.0%
R2000V 24.5%	S&P 500 2.1%	RESI [illegible]	R Mid V 33.5%	R1000G 13.1%	BC Gov/Cr 0.2%	Emerg Mkts 11.6%	R2000G 22.2%	R Mid G -4.8%	R Mid V 27.1%	R Mid V 12.4%
Emerg Mkts [illegible]	R1000V 0.4%	R1000V 17.5%	R1000V 32.5%	R Mid G 11.9%	R Mid G -0.2%	Cmmdty 11.4%	S&P 500 21.8%	RESI [illegible]	R1000V 26.5%	RESI [illegible]
R1000G 16.7%	Cmmdty -1.2%	S&P 500 16.0%	S&P 500 32.4%	BC Gov/Cr 6.0%	MS EAFE -0.4%	R2000G 11.3%	R1000V 13.7%	R1000V -8.3%	RESI [illegible]	R1000V 11.8%
R1000V 15.5%	R Mid V -1.4%	R Mid G 15.8%	MS EAFE 23.3%	R2000G 5.6%	R2000G -1.4%	RESI [illegible]	R Mid V 13.3%	R2000G -9.3%	MS EAFE 22.7%	R2000V 10.6%
S&P 500 15.1%	R Mid G -1.7%	R1000G 15.3%	RESI [illegible]	R2000V 4.2%	R1000V -3.8%	R Mid G 7.3%	R2000V 7.8%	R Mid V -12.3%	R2000V 22.4%	MS EAFE 6.0%
Cmmdty 9.0%	R2000G -2.9%	R2000G 14.6%	BC Inter Gov/Cr [illegible]	BC Inter Gov/Cr [illegible]	R Mid V -4.8%	R1000G 7.1%	Cmmdty 5.8%	R2000V -12.9%	Emerg Mkts [illegible]	Emerg Mkts [illegible]
MS EAFE 8.2%	R2000V -5.5%	BC Gov/Cr 4.8%	Cmmdty -1.2%	Emerg Mkts [illegible]	R2000V -7.5%	BC Gov/Cr 3.1%	RESI [illegible]	MS EAFE -13.4%	Cmmdty 17.6%	BC Gov/Cr 4.0%
BC Gov/Cr 6.6%	MS EAFE -11.7%	BC Inter Gov/Cr [illegible]	Emerg Mkts [illegible]	MS EAFE -4.5%	Emerg Mkts [illegible]	BC Inter Gov/Cr [illegible]	BC Gov/Cr 4.0%	Cmmdty -13.8%	BC Gov/Cr 9.7%	BC Inter Gov/Cr [illegible]
BC Inter Gov/Cr [illegible]	Emerg Mkts [illegible]	Cmmdty 0.1%	BC Gov/Cr -2.4%	Cmmdty -33.1%	Cmmdty -32.9%	MS EAFE 1.5%	BC Inter Gov/Cr [illegible]	Emerg Mkts [illegible]	BC Inter Gov/Cr [illegible]	Cmmdty -5.4%

Past performance is no guarantee of future results. You may not invest directly in an index. Generally, among asset classes stocks are more volatile than bonds or short-term instruments. Foreign investments involve greater risk than US investments as it depends upon currency values, political and regulatory environments, and overall market and economic factors of other countries. The following indices were used to represent the asset classes in this chart: International - MSCI EAFE, Emerging Markets - MSCI Emerging Markets, Small Growth - Russell 2000 Growth, Large Core - S&P 500, Small Value - Russell 2000 Value, Large Growth - Russell 1000 Growth, Interm Gov/Cr - Barclays Capital Intermediate U.S. Government/Credit, Gov/Cr - Barclays Capital U.S. Government/Credit, Large Value - Russell 1000 Value, Real Estate - Wilshire RESI, Commodity - S&P GSCI, Mid Value - Russell Midcap Value, Mid Growth - Russell Midcap Growth

TAKING THE EMOTION OUT OF INVESTING

Understanding the emotional cycle that takes place in investing will help you recognize the need to learn how to take the emotions out of your investing strategies and set up key performance indicators (KPIs) that dictate how you will invest without the emotional rollercoaster. Below is how our minds and emotions work as we invest. You can see that this is not an effective way to invest your money, time, or emotions. Learning to be analytical rather than emotional about how you invest will save you thousands of dollars and help you sleep better at night.

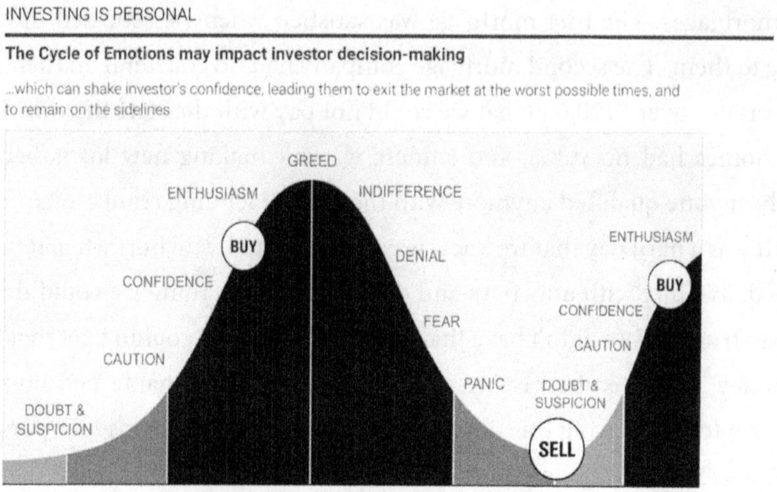

UNDERSTANDING YOUR RISK TOLERANCE LEVEL

I understand that you can't make money without losing money. I have survived poor investments and lived to tell the tale. My husband and I got into the real estate market in 2006. In 2007, we did our research and decided to build a half-million-dollar spec home. It was at the height of the housing market, home prices were through the roof, and we felt we were in a good position to make a good profit. Unfortunately, halfway through the construction process in 2008, the housing market crashed across the country overnight. We were in the middle of building, the house was no longer worth what we were building it for, and we were paying over $100 per day in construction loan interest. We had to finish the house and move it into long-term financing quickly. We tried to sell it, but no one could get a loan at that time with the mortgage lending collapse that happened at the same time. We ended up giving the house back to the bank. We knew there would be ramifications but didn't know what they would be or when they would hit us.

The day after Thanksgiving, we received a knock at our door. When I opened the door, a Sheriff stood there and handed me papers. We were being served papers that the second mortgage lender was suing us for non-payment. You see, when we refinanced out of the construction loan, we rolled it into two mortgages. The first mortgage was satisfied when we returned the spec home to them. The second mortgage company had no collateral on their loan and was out over $100,000 that we could not pay with the state the world was in – homes had no value, and lenders weren't making new loans because hardly anyone qualified anymore with the stricter lending regulations.

It was a hard day that we knew was coming, but it still hurt when it finally arrived. We met with attorneys and deemed the only thing we could do was file bankruptcy. We didn't have that kind of money and couldn't get that kind of money. It was embarrassing, and a lot of guilt and shame tied into this situation for us. During this time, we lost the spec home, we lost our personal home, our retirement, and our credit.

We took our kids and found a place to rent. It wasn't nearly as nice as our personal home had been, and our marriage took a significant hit during this time. We were on the verge of divorce and were not in a good place for several years. We moved several times over the next eight years, and it was hard on our kids — changing schools, making new friends, etc. The "good" news, if you could call it that, was that we were not alone. It's a staggering and sobering number to know that over six million Americans lost their homes to foreclosure during the great recession and housing crisis that started in 2008 (Ohlrogge, 2021).

Friends, family, and even strangers who heard about our situation would ask us if we do it again. My husband was an emphatic no, while I was an emphatic yes! Though this was the hardest and darkest time in our marriage and for our family, I learned so much from the process and the experience that I would definitely do it again… *just differently*. That is the blessing of experience. Hopefully, we will learn and grow from such experiences.

Investing isn't for the faint of heart — whether in the stock market, real estate, or business investments. You can see from the graph above that poor decisions are made in the heat of the moment if you make them with your emotions. You need to go into investing with a strategy and a game plan. You also need to have a good understanding of your risk tolerance and, if you are married, what your spouse's risk tolerance is to make decisions that you can both live with.

When I work with clients, I take a holistic approach to understand their goals and values, how much time they have left to invest before they want to retire, and of course, their risk tolerance for investing. I use Charles Schwab's investor profile questionnaire with my clients. It asks great questions and provides a good visual of their results. A link at the end of the chapter allows you to test your own risk tolerance.

You aren't going to invest the majority of your money in bonds, which are usually considered safe money and used to diversify risk if you have lots of time left to invest and have a high tolerance for risk. And you're surely not going to hop straight into the market with no investment education and a low tolerance for risk. Understanding your values, goals, timing, and risk tolerance level helps you create a more successful and realistic investment strategy to meet your current and future needs.

As you evaluate each of these criteria, you can see that your investment strategy will and should change over the years. When you are younger, have more time to invest, and can better rebuild your portfolio from losses, you will most likely take higher risks initially. However, as you get older, have less time before you want to retire, and have money you want to protect, your investment strategies will change to less risky investments to ensure you don't lose all that you have worked for over the years. Working with a financial advisor can help you think through the ways you can put your money to work toward your personal and financial goals at the appropriate time.

"Being disciplined as an investor isn't always easy, but over time it has demonstrated the ability to generate wealth...," observes Ann Dowd, CFP®, vice president at Fidelity Investments. "Having a plan that includes appropriate asset allocation and regular rebalancing can help investors overcome this challenge."

Investing is essential for building wealth over the long term, but it also involves some degree of risk. You must conduct thorough research and analysis before investing, including understanding the potential risks and returns of the investment, the market conditions, and the underlying economic factors that can impact the investment.

Diversification is a key strategy for managing investment risk by spreading investments across different asset classes, sectors, and regions. Having a long-term investment strategy that aligns with personal financial goals and risk tolerance is also important.

Investing also requires discipline, patience, and emotional control. Investors should avoid making impulsive decisions based on market fluctuations or news headlines and should stick to their long-term investment plans. It is also important to regularly monitor and review investment portfolios and make adjustments as necessary.

Investing is crucial for achieving financial goals and building wealth over time, but it requires education, planning, and a long-term perspective.

RESOURCES

Charles Schwab Investor Profile Questionnaire

Schedule a free, no-obligation appointment to review your personal finances and discuss your investment strategies to reach your goals

BOOK RECOMMENDATIONS

The Power of Zero, by David McKnight

ACTION MAP

1. Work through all the exercises for this chapter in the *Go For It!* Companion Workbook

2. Watch the Power of Zero documentary
3. Analyze your risk tolerance level with the Charles Schwab Investor Profile Questionnaire
4. Schedule a free, no-obligation appointment to review your personal finances and discuss your investment strategies to reach your goals
5. Read *The Power of Zero*

* I'd like to thank Elysium Financial (https://www.myelysium.com) for permission to use these images and many of the statistics for this chapter.

** 37% is the highest tax bracket in 2021.

To learn more about Elysium, follow the link below.

CHAPTER TEN

Your Dream Life Financial Tools

"Dreams don't work unless you do."
– John C. Maxwell

It's time to get to work! We've gone through the mindset work; now it's time to learn the skill set that will really allow you to fly. It's time to let go of everything weighing you down. And for most people, 70-90% of what is holding them down is their finances. The tools I will outline in this chapter will create a solid map that will help you see where you're at right now, support your Dream Life Plan, and allow you to accelerate and continue on your journey to everything you want to DO, HAVE and BECOME.

Each of these tools should be used in tandem to maximize your success. Follow the plan, and you will reap your rewards.

Each tool discussed here can be found at the link at the end of this chapter. Each tool has training video(s) on how to use it effectively and see the most results. The Dream Life Plan tools include:

THE EXPENSE TRACKER

A friend and I were at lunch, and she was really upset about money. She and her husband made good money but were always broke. She couldn't understand it. She was frustrated because her husband had accused her of being the reason they were broke. She was near tears as she went through what she spent their money on – groceries, things for the kids when needed, and she splurged once or twice a week for a $3 tea at Starbucks. She couldn't see how that was driving them to the poor house.

I asked her if she would use my expense tracker for 30 days to determine where her money was going. She said she would. I sent it to her later that day. I explained to her that she had to track EVERY PENNY spent. It didn't matter where the money came from – their paychecks, birthday money, change from the couch — she had to track it.

Thirty days later, my friend called me crying. She diligently tracked all their money and found out she was spending over $500 a month at Starbucks!! She couldn't believe it. In her mind, she was only spending $3 once or twice per week, when in reality, she was going five to six times per week, and she was spending way more than $3 on each visit. Sure, she got her tea, but she usually had her kids with her, so there were treats, lemonades, and other items on each order.

I told her she could keep $100 in cash each month for her trips to Starbucks, and when the money was gone, it was gone until the next month. She would need to be judicious about when she went and how much she spent each time. We took the other $400+ she had been spending and directed her to pay down their credit card debt. Within a few months, they paid down a significant amount of debt with that extra $400!

It's funny how our mind plays tricks on us. I can't tell you how often I have worked with clients who "KNEW" where their money was going until I had them actually track it. Most come back after 30 days, shocked to learn where their money was really going.

Don't let the simplicity of this tool fool you. It's powerful if you use it. It's powerful if you're honest with yourself and your spouse if you're married. It's powerful to provide insights, allowing you to make huge changes in handling your money.

You have a dream right now. You're passionate about it, and you want to go after it. You're just trying to figure out how to pay for it. Many clients find they have more expendable money than they thought they had. They just need to find it and redirect it to what they really want.

The DLP Expense Tracker will show you where the leaks are on your boat. We want to identify the leaks and plug them up before you start drowning. I encourage you to download the Expense Tracker and track how you spend every penny today!

THE DREAM LIFE PLANNER

I worked with one of my first clients about 16 years ago. The wife had reached out to me. They were drowning in medical bill debt. Their son had a rare disease and was always in and out of the hospital. They both had decent jobs, but they had already been living paycheck to paycheck before all the medical bills started pouring in. When we started working together, they had almost $60,000 in outstanding medical bills that needed to be paid, with more coming.

I got on my first call with them to review their new budget. It was clear the husband was not happy with his wife for reaching out to me. This was before video conferencing, and we were just on the phone. Even through the phone, I could feel the tension and hear his frustration. His wife had previously sent me all their financial information, and I had created a budget for them to start living with that would allow them to start making payments on the medical bills. The husband was getting increasingly upset as I started going through the budget. I showed them where their money ran out before the month's end based on how they were spending it. The husband spent about $100 each month stopping at the gas station for sodas and treats every day on his way to work. I suggested that habits needed to change in order to start paying down some of the medical bills.

OH MY GOSH! That poor man exploded on that call! He was indignant and told me he NEEDED his soda each day. Having cash in his pocket was very important to him and allowed him to feel like a man. He said a few things to me and then hung up the phone. I waited a couple of minutes and called him back, and asked him if he felt better. He was contrite, and I asked him if I could finish the plan and see if he could still have his soda every day. We did finish the call, I showed him how he could still have his soda every day. It just didn't include going to the gas station every day. They agreed to start working on the plan we outlined together.

I am very proud to say that they worked very hard and managed to pay off all those medical bills, get completely out of debt, and stay out of debt! And that husband became my greatest proponent! He sent more clients to me than anyone else over the years! LOL. His testimonial is one of my favorites!

> *"I hated you! There, I said it! I hated your program. I hated my wife for signing us up to work with Donna. I hated that Donna made me look at what I was really doing to my family by spending what I was spending on myself each month. I hated working on my "money mindset." I thought the exercises were hokey. I hated that she was so *!@& nice about it even when I was a jerk. I hung up on her once – she just called me back and asked if I felt better. Talk about feeling like a heel. It's now been five years since we worked with her, and we are still out of debt. I know now that those exercises that I hated so much are what changed our lives. I don't hate many things anymore. I definitely don't hate Donna anymore. I can't thank her (and my wife) enough for being patient with me. I was a stubborn idiot for a long time. But I'm not anymore. I am in a better place financially and emotionally." – R.B., Idaho*

When you open up the Dream Life Planner tool, you may think, "This is just a budget worksheet!" And you know what? You're not wrong! But you're not right either.

This tool will put the power of money in your control for once. As the saying goes, "If you don't control your money, it will control you." I want to put YOU in control of your money. You are going to give every dollar you earn a job. You are going to tell your money that you are now the boss. You get to start designing YOUR Dream Life Plan right this minute!

The Dream Life Planner will identify WHAT you need to pay each month. You'll see that it is set up in a specific order to make sure your basic needs are covered first. If there is still money left over, you can pay down debt, then enjoy the extra things in life. If there isn't enough money, it's the extra things in life that need to be set aside to ensure you have a roof over your head, food in your kitchen, clothing on your back, and your family is provided for each month.

This is a zero-balance budget. That means you will assign every dollar each month. You're not looking for a surplus. You're looking to direct your money into your needs first and then your wants.

While many people dread this part, after they do it and see where they are at, whether good or bad, they are thrilled to finally "see" where they are at. Most people bury their heads in the sand and just fly by the seat of their pants. But not you! You have a dream to go after, and you recognize this is just a tool to get you to your dream faster.

THE DREAM LIFE CASH FLOW PLANNER

One of my clients made a LOT of money but was extremely frustrated that there was never enough "FUN" money for the family. They couldn't understand why. They were bringing in almost $200,000 per year and felt broke. I started reviewing their finances. As I went through their bank statement, I nearly choked as I calculated they were spending almost $800 per month on insufficient funds charges each month! How in the world was that even possible?!?!?

I was stymied for a while as I kept working on their finances. On our next call, I asked them what was going on? They told me that each account was set up on automatic payments that just didn't hit their bank at the right time. What?!!? Talk about giving up control of your own money! I had them cancel every single auto payment over the next couple of days. We used the Dream

Life Cash Flow Planner to identify when everything needed to be paid and which check was being used to pay it. They never had an NSF charge again and they immediately saw an $800 increase to their budget and had LOTS of fun money to play and travel with each month.

It's important to not give others control of your money. The Dream Life Cash Flow Planner is going to identify WHEN you need to spend your money each month. Most people spend way too much time fretting about paying their bills on time and worrying about when each bill is due and sometimes miss paying a bill because it's due at a random time during the month when they aren't thinking about their finances.

The Dream Life Cash Flow Planner saves you time and mental energy. You only worry about your bills the day you get paid. It already has everything broken down into what you are paying with each paycheck. There is no more trying to calculate how much to spend on that check because you've already done the work.

THE DREAM LIFE DEBT ELIMINATOR

We had just filled out the Dream Life Debt Eliminator. It was all there in black and white, and it was not pretty. $432,652. They sat there in stone-cold silence. No words. No tears. Just shock. Even if you take out the mortgage, it was a stunning number. $183,647. The wife started to stutter, "How?!" The husband just hung his head. Another few minutes of silence went by. I needed them to feel the pain. I needed them to recognize where they were at right this minute. I wasn't there to sugar coat it, offer them platitudes that it was okay or that it would be easy – it wouldn't – or to cheer them on… yet. They had to feel the pain to understand and appreciate when the pain was gone. We sat for another few minutes. When I saw tears rolling down the wife's face, I spoke.

"It is what it is. It's not pretty, it's downright ugly and scary, but there is nothing we can do about it now. It's time to throw down the shovels that you keep using to dig yourselves into a deeper and deeper hole and start climbing your way back out."

We lined up the debt in order from the lowest balance to the highest. In this case, it was a loan to a family member all the way up to their mortgage. They had money in their budget to pay off part of the loan. They could pay off the balance in two more months. Once they paid off the loan, we took the money they used the last three months ($150) and applied it to the next largest debt, a credit card. The $150 amount plus the $42 minimum payment they were making went to that credit card until it was paid off. Once it was paid off, that $192 was added to the minimum payment on the next card of $77.

Making $269 payments instead of $77 makes a much larger dent in the balance. You can see it dropping faster and faster. You get motivated! You want to throw every dollar you can at it, and so that is what we do. Any extra dollar we throw at the debt. Tax refunds, bonuses, even Christmas and birthday money sometimes, depending on your desires.

Whenever I get in my car, I turn on the GPS to where I'm going if it's over 10 miles, even if I've been there 100 times. I'm not looking for directions. I'm looking at how long it says it's going to take to get there. And then I think, "I can beat that!" For the record, I'm not a speed demon! I'm not! I don't go out there and pretend to be racing the Indy 500. I just value my time and look for faster ways of doing things.

The Debt Eliminator works the same way as the GPS. Once you add ALL of your debt, you can clearly see how long it will take to pay everything off. I love it when people get the vision and say, "We can beat that!" It becomes a challenge. It becomes addicting. It becomes a mission for your family.

When we entered their debt into the Debt Eliminator, it showed 22 years with their mortgage. When we took out the mortgage, it showed it would take nine years. UGH!! Who wants to scrimp, save, and go without for NINE years?!?! I don't! They didn't! I showed them how throwing an extra $100 a month would pay it down in eight years. I showed them that throwing their tax refund for just one year would take it down to six years. They got it! They saw how powerful throwing extra dollars at it exponentially dropped the length of time it would take! They went back to their budget and made some adjustments. They reevaluated where their money was going and were able to pull another $180 per month from the budget to add to the debt they owed.

The Expense Tracker may be eye-opening, but the Debt Eliminator is motivating! It could be depressing at first as you write down and calculate ALL of your debt. When you see it there in black and white it can feel like an insurmountable feat to get all that paid off, especially as you look at what you make and how tight things feel already. But don't fret!! This IS doable! Remember when we discussed vision boards, declarations, and help from sources known and unknown? THIS is one of those areas where all those come into play.

That is how it worked for this couple. They had money come to them in ways that were miraculous and after everything was paid off other than their mortgage, it took them THREE years! Three years instead of nine! That's incredible! Once they paid that off, they threw everything at their mortgage and paid that off in four years. Seven years in total instead of 22 years! That's FIFTEEN years ahead of schedule! And that, my friends, is a huge blessing!

"Remember, all work works! When it doesn't work *for* us, it works *on* us. And the work our work does for us is always more important than the work it does for us. The work it does for us increases our commodities, but the work it does on us increases our capacity!" – Myron Golden

RESOURCES

Dream Life Plan financial tools. Each tool has a video training on how to use it.

BOOK RECOMMENDATIONS

Financial Peace by Dave Ramsey

ACTION MAP

1. Work through all the exercises for this chapter in the *Go For It!* Companion Workbook.
2. Use the Expense Tracker to track every expense for the next 30 days to determine where your money is actually going.
3. Use the Dream Life Planner to determine *how* to spend your money.
4. Use the Cash Flow Worksheet to determine *when* to spend your money.
5. Use the Debt Eliminator to identify your debt and create a game plan to pay it off as fast as you can.
6. Read *Financial Peace.*

CHAPTER ELEVEN

Life is a Highway

"Do you start feeling down near the end of the year when you think about the goals you will miss? I know I do. A good friend and I were chatting about this the other day, and he reminded me of something: Achieving your goals is a lot like taking a road trip. The further you have to go (aka the bigger the goal), the more times you need to refuel. The more pit stops you need to make. But that's OK! You wouldn't consider a cross-country trip a failure because you needed to refill the tank, right? So why consider yourself a failure when you need to refill your own tank? It's just a part of the journey." **— Paul Shin, Lover of Tacos**

CELEBRATING WINS ALONG THE WAY

Humans are naturally wired to focus on the end goal, the finish line, and the ultimate outcome. While it's important to have a clear destination in mind, we often overlook the journey's significance. The journey is where we learn, grow, and develop the skills necessary to achieve our goals. Celebrating wins along the journey is essential because it reminds us of our progress and motivates us to continue pushing forward.

Celebrating wins helps us to recognize and acknowledge our achievements. It's easy to get lost in the day-to-day struggles and forget just how far we've come. By taking the time to celebrate small milestones, we gain a sense of accomplishment and boost our self-esteem. Celebrating wins also helps us to see the bigger picture and how each small step leads us closer to our goal. When we take a moment to reflect on our progress, we are reminded that we are on the right path, and it's worth continuing to move forward.

Celebrating wins along the journey helps to maintain motivation and momentum. It's easy to become discouraged when we're working toward a long-term goal. The journey can be grueling, and it's not uncommon to experience setbacks and challenges along the way. Celebrating wins, no matter how small, reminds us that progress is being made and that our efforts are paying off. This sense of progress and accomplishment helps to keep us motivated and focused on our goals.

Celebrating wins creates positive momentum and can lead to even greater success. When we take the time to recognize and celebrate our wins, we create a positive feedback loop. This positive momentum can propel us forward, leading to even greater achievements. Celebrating wins creates a sense of optimism and confidence, which can lead to new opportunities and possibilities.

Celebrating wins can also help to create a sense of community and connection. Sharing our successes with others can inspire and motivate them to achieve their goals. Celebrating wins with friends, family, or colleagues creates a sense of camaraderie and shared purpose. We can create a positive and supportive environment that fosters growth and development by celebrating wins together.

And finally, celebrating wins along the journey is essential for success. Recognizing and acknowledging our achievements helps to maintain motivation, create positive momentum, and keep us focused on our goals. Celebrating wins also creates a sense of community and connection, which can lead to even greater success. So, whether big or small, take the time to celebrate your wins and enjoy the journey toward your goals.

THE IMPORTANCE OF MAINTAINING YOUR VEHICLE

Maintaining your vehicle is important to make sure you reach your destination. Regular maintenance ensures that your vehicle is in good working condition and reduces the risk of accidents. Regular inspections can catch potential problems before they turn into major safety hazards. The most dangerous hazard on the road is a vehicle that is not maintained.

I was driving up to Sun Valley, Idaho, for a conference years ago. I was three cars behind a truck with a camper shell on it. All of a sudden, the camper shell came off the truck on a narrow bridge. There was nowhere to swerve because of the concrete barrier. The first car behind the truck took the biggest hit as it hit their windshield, and they swerved into the barrier. The second car drove over the camper shell now on the road and broke it up into pieces. When I hit that camper shell, I felt and heard the pieces scraping my car and hitting the undercarriage. There was nowhere for me to stop for miles and my car appeared to be running fine, so I kept going on my trip (I don't recommend you doing that!) I was about 100 miles north of the accident when I stopped for gas and finally took a look at my car. It was pretty bad. My car was scraped up all the way down the driver's side. The front bumper had been pulled off a bit, but was okay to drive. I called the Utah Highway Patrol and told them what had happened and that I needed to file a report. The dispatcher told me the officer in charge would call me to take my report. I still hadn't heard from the officer three days later and called again. When he picked up, he apologized and told me that over 100 vehicles had been damaged somehow from that camper falling off. I finally got my car repaired to like new, but it took six weeks. I can't imagine the insurance carrier kept them as clients after the damage they caused and the filed claims and the payouts they had to make.

You need to maintain your vehicle when you are on your journey to go after your dreams. Not taking care of yourself will delay your journey. Entrepreneurs are notorious for working long hours, but it is counterintuitive.

You need to learn your optimal working schedule, do your heavy work during that time, and then do the rest during a normal schedule.

I am a morning person — like an EARLY morning person — a 4:30-5 a.m. morning person. I like to get up early and get the hardest things done that require my full attention before interruptions begin. When I was an employee, I worked for a manager whose optimal working time was late afternoon/early evening. I would get to work at 7 a.m., where I would find a pile of papers on my desk for things he needed me to get done. I would have everything done when he came in around 9 a.m. Then the office got busy, and I dealt with normal office interruptions. Then when it got quiet, he was able to take the work that I had gotten done for him and do his heavy lifting during his peak time. It was a great synergy.

When I had my first business partner, we also had a great synergy. I was a dreamer and a starter, but she was a finisher and loved being organized. We worked well together and accomplished a lot.

I have learned over the years that if my vehicle isn't at its peak, my work is not either. I have learned the importance of setting boundaries for my working hours, the amount of sleep I get, the foods I eat, and what I drink. My mantra used to be that my plate was never full because I could run down to IKEA and get a bigger plate. I thought being busy was a badge of honor when it was burning me out, and I wasn't accomplishing nearly as much as I could if I took time to sharpen my saw.

Now, my priorities have changed. I only work on things that move the needle in my business and get me closer to my goals. Sleep is a priority. I don't drink soda or alcohol. I drink a gallon of water every day. I fuel my body with good food, not junk food, that gives me a quick fix and, ultimately, a hard crash. I have a hard boundary of the hours I work to make sure I have quality time with my family and I am fully present with them.

WHAT TO DO WHEN YOU HIT A POTHOLE

Life is full of surprises, some good and some bad. Sometimes, life throws you a curve ball that you never expected. It can be a challenging situation that leaves you feeling lost, confused, and unsure of how to move forward. But even in the face of adversity, there are steps you can take to regain control and find your way through.

The first step is to acknowledge the situation for what it is. Don't try to downplay it or pretend it's not happening. Accept that this is a difficult time and that you must work through it. This can be a tough pill to swallow, but moving forward is essential.

Next, take some time to reflect on your emotions. You may be feeling overwhelmed, angry, sad, or even numb. All of these emotions are valid and normal in response to a curve ball. Take time to process your feelings, but also try not to get lost in them. It's important to strike a balance between acknowledging your emotions and not letting them consume you.

Once you have processed your emotions, start to think about what you can do to move forward. This may involve seeking help or support from others. You don't have to face a curve ball alone. Reach out to friends, family, or even a professional if needed. Sometimes, talking to someone can help you gain perspective and find a way forward.

You may also need to re-evaluate your goals and priorities. A curve ball can force you to reassess what's important to you and what you want to achieve. Take the time to reflect on what you truly want and what steps you can take to get there.

Finally, take action. It can be easy to get stuck in a cycle of worry and uncertainty, but taking action can help you regain a sense of control. This could involve making a plan, taking small steps toward your goals, or simply focusing on self-care and self-improvement.

This book took me over two years to write because I hit several potholes over the course of time. I will NEVER write a book again the way I wrote this one. Again, I have learned from my trials and will improve the process next time.

When I started writing this book, I was working full-time, scaling my consulting business, and opening up my coaching business. I felt I could just write for an hour or two each morning before work while my family was sleeping so I wasn't taking more time away from them. I had heard other famous authors did the same thing, so it seemed like a great plan.

Then I started hitting potholes that delayed the completion of this book.

My Pothole #1 — Fear of Failure.

Do you remember in the introduction of this book where I told you about the classes I took in summer school for fun? One of the classes was creative writing. It was set up that there were different levels of writing that you had to pass to get to the next level. So I would submit a story each week, and each week, I wouldn't pass to the next level. The notes from the teacher said things such as… "not very believable," "not interesting enough," and "doesn't flow." I would get my paper back each week and feel horrible about myself as I read their notes.

These memories kept coming up for me as I wrote this book. I would ask myself, "Who am I to write this book?" And I worried that no one would be interested or even buy a copy. We had a game night with some friends and talked about books we had recently read. One of my friends mentioned that he didn't like the book and gave various reasons. It scared me that even if people bought the book, what if they didn't like it and then didn't like me? Remember, our brain will try to stop us in the pursuit of "protecting us," so I quit writing for a time.

A year later, I co-authored a book with Jim Britt, an award-winning author of 15 best-selling books and seven international best-sellers, and Kevin Harrington, the founder of As Seen on TV and was one of the original "Sharks" on the ABC TV series Shark Tank. The book became an international best-seller in over 40 categories. Instead of celebrating and enjoying the moment, my new fear became, "What if my personal book wasn't a best-seller?" How would I feel? How could I face that "failure"? Again, I had to work on my mindset. I had to realize I was writing this book with a genuine desire to help people go after their dreams successfully. I realized I was being selfish by letting my fears stop me from serving others. And really, what is the worst that would happen if it wasn't as big as the other book? And so, I finished my book.

My Pothole #2 — Losing Half of My Book

I finally finished my book and was ready to send it to the editor. I was so excited! I had completed a huge project and was thrilled. Then I opened my file to check it one last time before submitting it and realized over half of it was missing! I contacted two of my friends who were in IT and begged them to help me recover my document. I wrote my entire book in one MS Word document. I have used MS Word for over 20 years and have never had a file go corrupt. Each one of them went through my computer and tried different things, including rolling back the date on my machine. Nothing. I had lost over half of my book. I cried. I UGLY cried. I had to come to terms with the fact that I needed to start over and rewrite several chapters and various things in the other chapters. I was deflated, and it took me several months to get the motivation to rewrite. What did help me, though, was knowing that others knew about my book and would ask me about how it was coming. This was peer pressure at its finest, and I was so grateful for it because I just couldn't, and I didn't have it in me to say, "I decided not to finish it." And so I did!

A note about me: I use humor to get me through hard things. And so I made a joke about the loss of so much. My husband and I are bowlers. One year we were bowling together in a co-ed league. One night we were bowling against a Polynesian team. There was a cute lady on their team who kept saying, "Your first bowler, suuuuuuuuuuucks!" It was hilarious because, thankfully, I wasn't our first bowler. It was funny because of her accent. It was funny because of how she drew out the word sucks! And so I joked that those chapters I lost just "suuuuuuuuuuuucked" and needed to be rewritten.

Needless to say, I made MULTIPLE copies after that. I created a new Google Drive Document for each chapter and managed them separately until I was done, then combined each document into one full book when all the chapters were completed.

My Pothole #3 — Nearly Losing My Consulting Firm

While COVID-19 hit the world in 2020, our firm wasn't affected until 2022, when the supply chain issues hit our firm. We only had one new sale in the entire year of 2021 because our clients had no idea if or when they would have clients come back to work. It was because we were financially sound and had an emergency fund and credit available to us that we survived that year and most of 2022. It was the third quarter of 2022 when we realized we had to make drastic decisions to keep the firm going. Needless to say, the stress of working on saving the firm made me stop writing the book. Not for long, but enough to make it hard to get started again. But I did it.

I had some major setbacks in completing this book. Some I created on my own. Some were out of my control. But always, I fought back and am proud to say this book is now published, and you are reading it!

Remember that every journey may have a pothole or two or four. It's how you respond to them that makes all the difference. You can find a way through even the most challenging situations by acknowledging the situation, processing your emotions, seeking support, re-evaluating your goals, and taking action.

TAKE TIME TO REFUEL AND RECHARGE YOURSELF

Refueling and recharging are essential to achieving any long-term goal because they help you maintain your physical and mental well-being. Pursuing a goal over an extended period of time can be physically and mentally draining, which is why taking time to recharge is critical.

When you refuel, you give your body the energy it needs to keep going. This means getting enough sleep, eating a healthy diet, and staying hydrated. Without proper nutrition and rest, your body will not be able to function at its best, making it difficult for you to stay focused and productive.

Recharging means engaging in activities that help you relax and reduce stress. This can include anything from walking in nature to practicing meditation or yoga or just enjoying time with family and friends. When you take time to recharge, you give your mind a break from the constant demands of pursuing a long-term goal. This can help you stay motivated and focused in the long run.

Overall, refueling and recharging are important because they help you maintain the physical and mental stamina necessary to achieve your goals. By taking care of yourself, you can stay motivated, focused, and productive, even when pursuing a challenging goal.

Cars is one of my favorite Pixar films. My kids were young when it came out, so I can honestly say I have seen it well over 100 times, even though it's been a while. Part of the movie's message is to slow down and enjoy the ride. Most of us are so intent on arriving at our destination that we don't slow down to enjoy the journey. We just keep watching the clock to see how long it takes to get there.

The town of Kanab, Utah, was the inspiration for Radiator Springs. The red rock and green pines are even more picturesque than they are in the movie. The highway in the film is just like I-15 — long, straight, and full of sagebrush. But just a short distance off I-15 just East of Panguitch, Utah, there is another canyon that looks exactly like Radiator Springs: red rock and green pine. If you are ever traveling through Utah, I highly recommend taking a little side trip and heading up the canyon from exit 95 to Highway UT-20 just north of Parowan to Red Canyon Visitor Center. There are a couple of easy walking trails that are completely worth your time.

The journey toward achieving our dreams can be long and challenging, but it's important to keep going and celebrate the small wins along the way.

It's also important to avoid the potholes, if at all possible, that can derail our progress and take care of ourselves physically, mentally, and emotionally. By slowing down and enjoying the journey, we can find meaning and fulfillment in pursuing our dreams.

BOOK RECOMMENDATIONS

You've Got This! by Will Matthews

ACTION MAP

1. Work through all the exercises for this chapter in the *Go For It!* Companion Workbook
2. Read *You've Got This!*

A NOTE ABOUT PAUL SHIN

I started following Paul Shin on LinkedIn a couple of years ago. He was connected to several people I know and respect. And really, how can you not love a guy who signs his name, taco lover, with a taco emoji?!? I recently met Paul in person over lunch. Sadly, no, we did not go out for tacos, but I did get to learn more about his story and his movement, Tacos Together. He is a genuinely kind person who wants to help others find their community. His story is inspiring. I hope you'll take a moment to learn about Paul and his organization, Tacos Together. Here is a podcast interview with Paul.

A blurb about the Podcast:

Paul Shin is a builder. He is a builder of community. He is a builder of people. He also knows how to build tacos. The bottom line, things are better together with Paul! We are all inspired by the way that Paul has been building and bringing the startup and tech communities together here in Utah!

Like all entrepreneurs, Paul Shin has been through the wringer. After making the decision to live, he took a path that has led him to meet so many incredible people and helped him discover the power of genuine human connection.

Paul is one of the founders of Tacos Together @thetacostogetherpodcast; they make it fun and easy to make human connections through the events they organize.

One of the events that Paul helped organize in 2022 ultimately set a world record for the largest blanket fort ever constructed, covering 10,000 square feet! Those blankets ended up being donated to homeless shelters. This is the caliber of cool things Paul is doing for people. Humans have the innate desire to connect with other humans, and Paul is making that easier for us all.

We hope you enjoy this conversation! Follow him on social media to keep up with upcoming events!

- LinkedIn: https://www.linkedin.com/in/thepaulshin/
- Instagram: https://www.instagram.com/tacos_together/
- Website: https://tacostogether.com/

Podcast video courtesy of Lemonade Stand Stories Podcast
https://www.youtube.com/@lemonadestandstories

CHAPTER TWELVE

The True Meaning of Living Your Life on Purpose

Living your life on purpose is about intentionally and consciously directing your actions and decisions toward a meaningful and fulfilling life. It means understanding your values, passions, and strengths and aligning them with your actions to create a sense of purpose and fulfillment.

Living your life on purpose requires self-awareness and reflection. It requires you to ask yourself the tough questions: What do I truly value in life? What brings me joy and fulfillment? What are my strengths, and how can I use them to contribute to the world? It's important to take the time to reflect on these questions and explore your interests and passions. By doing so, you can better understand yourself and what you want out of life.

Once you have a clear sense of your values, passions, and strengths, aligning your actions with them is important. This means making intentional choices and decisions that align with your goals and values. For example, if you value family and relationships, you might choose to prioritize spending time with loved ones over working long hours at the office. Or if you're passionate about environmental issues, you might choose to volunteer for an organization that works to protect the planet.

Living your life on purpose also requires taking responsibility for your choices and actions. It means recognizing that you have the power to create your own reality and that you are responsible for your life's direction. This can be empowering, but it can also be challenging. It means accepting that there will be obstacles and setbacks along the way but that you have the strength and resilience to overcome them.

Living your life on purpose is not about achieving a specific goal or destination. It's about embracing the journey and finding fulfillment in the present moment. It's about living a life that is true to who you are, and that aligns with your values and passions.

Living your life on purpose is about being intentional, self-aware, and aligned with your values and passions. It's about taking responsibility for your choices and actions and embracing the journey toward a fulfilling life. Living your life purposefully means finding meaning, fulfillment, and happiness in every moment.

ACTION MAP

1. Work through all the exercises for this chapter in the *Go For It!* Companion Workbook

CHAPTER THIRTEEN

What's Next For You

MAYBE WE CAN HELP.

From these pages, you have learned how to create a solid foundation to go after your goals. We focused on mindset first because mindset is often considered more important than skillset because it is the foundation upon which skills are built. A person's mindset influences their beliefs, attitudes, and behaviors, which ultimately determine how they approach learning, problem-solving, and decision-making.

While skills are certainly important, they are not necessarily fixed and can be developed and improved over time. However, a person's mindset can either facilitate or hinder their ability to develop new skills or adapt to changing circumstances.

For example, a person with a growth mindset believes that their abilities can be developed through dedication and hard work, while a person with a fixed mindset believes that their abilities are innate and unchangeable. A person with a growth mindset is more likely to persist through challenges and setbacks, and to actively seek out opportunities to learn and grow. This mindset is particularly important in today's rapidly changing and unpredictable world, where the ability to learn and adapt is critical to success.

In contrast, a person with a fixed mindset may be more likely to give up when faced with challenges and may be less open to feedback and new ideas.

This can limit their ability to learn and grow, and ultimately limit their potential for success.

Therefore, while skills are certainly important, mindset is the foundation upon which skills are built, and can ultimately determine a person's ability to learn, adapt, and succeed.

Perhaps you've never had the opportunity to go after a big goal or life's dream. There may be a lot you don't know about the process. That's where we come in.

Helping people like you is what we do day in and day out at Life on Purpose Academy.

The academy is where dreams and goals are achieved. Where businesses scale. Where generational wealth is created. With coaching and training and a community to champion you and give you resources and feedback along the way.

Is the academy right for you?

Maybe. Let's see.

If there is any part of you that feels that you could find success so much faster with our help than alone, perhaps we should chat.

Sometimes you can't see the forest for the trees, you can't see the whole situation clearly because you're looking too closely at small details or because you're too closely involved. It's easy to get stuck and lose steam or experience self-doubt even if you have a high-level road map in front of you as we created here with this book.

If you are excited about going after your goals and creating your dream life but it feels too big or too lonely, I have a suggestion.

Sign up for a free exploratory call so we can talk about your dreams. Sometimes all you need is a little nudge in the right direction to get going. Sometimes you might want a little more than that. We have been where you are now and understand exactly where you might be experiencing challenges and who can help you with your plan of action while also exploring with you what it would look like working together. Book your free session at: https://calendly.com/lifeonpurposeacademyut/clarity

If you are already in the middle of your journey - but burning out, worried if you'll ever make it, wondering where to go from here, or looking to figure out how to enjoy the journey more — you will find this exploratory call very helpful.

Time and time again, I've found that just one conversation can change your life for the better. This may be it. We offer a safe space to discuss your goals and dreams that you hesitate to share with anyone else. We're here with a compassionate ear to listen to your particular struggles — with zero judgment because we've been there too — and to help you find out what's slowing you down.

Go to https://calendly.com/lifeonpurposeacademyut/clarity and request the free session by answering a few simple questions. These will help us be better prepared to help you individually and give you better details on how we can help.

Your Roadmap for Your Dream Life Plan

Here is a quick summary of your roadmap for everything you want to create YOUR Dream Life Plan.

1. Create your dream list of everything you want to do, have, or become.
2. DECIDE! You've made your list… Now, decide your number one goal and create the roadmap to achieve it.
3. Create the list of steps it's going to take to reach your goal. Break those steps down further into manageable tasks.
4. Make a list of everyone you need to get on board with your goal and have those discussions.
5. Work on your mindset throughout your journey.
6. Create a solid financial foundation to reach your goal.
7. Enjoy the journey!
8. Celebrate the small wins along the way!
9. Be proud of yourself for reaching your goal!
10. Rinse and repeat with your next goal and your next one until you have created your ultimate dream life.

Resources

Appendix A

Companion Workbook

Go For It! Companion Workbook

Appendix B

People I Love to Work With

Richie Norton

Read the books, *The Power of Starting Something Stupid,* and *Anti-Time Management*

Sign up for this 76-Day Challenge to make your STUPID idea Your SMART Reality at

http://richienorton.com/76daychallenge/

Kirk and Kim Duncan

Check out his Master Your Influence group coaching at

https://3keyelements.com/master-your-influence-join-today/

Listen to any of his audiobook trainings at

https://3keyelements.com/audiobook-library/

Natasha Hazlett
Check her out at https://natashahazlett.com
Join her next 5-day Unstoppable Influence Challenge at
https://unstoppableInfluence.idevaffiliate.com/2194.html

Michael Yeung
Check out his website at https://www.eliteproductivity.io/
Join his free Facebook group at www.facebook.com/groups/teamppe

Appendix C

Complete List of Books I Recommend by Chapter

This section features affiliate links, meaning I will earn a small commission if you purchase through these links.

The Go-Giver by Bob Burg

The Richest Man in Babylon by George S. Clason

The Power of Starting Something Stupid by Richie Norton

How to Win Friends and Influence People by Dale Carnegie

Crucial Conversations: Tools for Talking When Stakes are High by Kerry Patterson

Unstoppable Influence: Be You. Be Fearless. Transform Lives. by Natasha Hazlett

The Perfect Day Formula by Craig Ballantyne

The 15 Invaluable Laws of Growth: Live Them and Reach Your Potential by John C. Maxwell

Attitude 101 by John C Maxwell

The Truth About Money by Ric Edelman

Rich Dad Poor Dad, Robert Kiyosaki

The Power of Zero, by David McKnight

Financial Peace by Dave Ramsey

You've Got This! by Will Matthews

Additional books I love that will help you on your journey

Anti-Time Management by Richie Norton

Psycho-Cybernetics by Maxwell Maltz

Appendix D

Other Links Included Throughout the Book

Chapter 3:

Video: Authenticity vs Attachment by Dr. Gabor Maté

Chapter 4:
Vision Board Training

Chapter 8:
The Power of Zero Documentary

Chapter 9:
Charles Schwab Investor Profile Questionnaire

Schedule a free, no-obligation appointment to review your personal finances and discuss your investment strategies to reach your goals here:

Chapter 10:

Dream Life Plan financial tools.

Each tool has a video training on how to use it.

THANK YOU FOR READING MY BOOK!

DOWNLOAD YOUR FREE GIFTS

Just to say thanks for buying and reading my book, I would like to give you a few free bonus gifts, no strings attached!

To Download Now, Visit:

www.go.lifeonpurposeacademy.com/GoForItBookGifts

I appreciate your interest in my book, and value your feedback as it helps me improve future versions. I would appreciate it if you could leave your invaluable review on Amazon.com with your feedback. Thank you!

Made in the USA
Monee, IL
04 November 2026

67378093R00105